Harold's Poetry

Harold's Poetry

Harold Franks

with help and encouragement
from friend, Carmel Smith

Title: Harold's Poetry

First published in 2025 by Kani Consultants, Newcastle, Australia.

© Copyright on the text belongs to the author, Harold Franks.

© Copyright on the collection belongs to Kani Consultants.

All rights reserved.

No part of this publication may be reproduced, stored in a retrieval system, or transmitted in any form by any means electronic, mechanical, photocopying, recording or otherwise without the prior consent of the publisher.

 A catalogue record for this work is available from the National Library of Australia

ISBN: 978-0-646-72530-7 Harold's Poetry

A note from the author:

Read this book for what it is:
a collection of poems about my life,
things I've seen, and what I've done.

My message to you *young ens* is this:
"Have a go at anything, don't give up."

Thank you to my good friend, Carmel Smith,
for your help and encouragement.

My Book

Within this book, I hope you'll find
A passage that will stretch your mind
For I have worked for quite some time
To bring to you both verse and rhyme

In my retirement, I've travelled some
Told some stories both sad and fun
Put some stories in this book
So turn the pages and have a look

With the covid running rife
Many people lost their life
Restrictions were put into place
I'm at home with a long face

With iPad and my stylus pen
Wrote some poems about it then
Took a liking to the works
Continued then with rhyme and verse

Adding pictures to the sets
Write on harbours, trees or vets
Anything that catches the eye
I see a verse and then I'll try

So readers of my book of words
Just like finding different birds
Some will appeal while others not
You won't know till you've read the lot.

150 Years On

One hundred and fifty years ago
A telegraph line began to grow
To snake its way across the land
Darwin to Adelaide it was bound

Twenty three months the workers toiled
Through monsoon rains and arid soil
Work they must, with axe and saw
Picks and shovels to the fore

Food was short, the way was rough
Work for those so fit and tough
Natives too, caused some pain
When they attacked on the open plain

Termites too, attacked the poles
While men were busy digging holes
Tree cutters on the axe and saw
Diggers calling for timbers, more and more

Finally finished, with cables laid
Morse Code then was to be played
Across the land and oceans deep
To celebrate an amazing feat

Today the morse has gone to sleep
No more dots and dashes keep
But to the morse men of the past
GN to all, may you rest at last.

A Bad Night

Off early to bed to read my book
Didn't help, I was feeling quite crook
Took two pills, to settle down
Neatly and snug neath my eiderdown

Finally off into a drug type sleep
Sticky and sweaty but sleep so deep
Into the land of nod, I went
Feeling my life was almost spent

Into the land of frightening dreams
Knocking noises and lots of screams
Heard a siren, soon awoke
Do I detect the smell of smoke?

My smoke alarm is what I hear
The house on fire is what I fear
Off to the toilet, tripped over the dog
I consider my mind is in a fog

The alarm goes on for three more beats
Settles down and goes to sleep
I fully wake on the toilet seat
Must go back to bed, I feel dead beat.

A Bag of Bones

I'm not just skin and a bag of bones
I have feelings, no heart of stones
Knowledge have I by the score
But no one asks me any more

The depression, as a baby, I went through
Second war, through it, I grew
Schooling days, I passed my test
Gave it all my very best

Took a wife and family, two
Watched the young ones, before they flew
Worked my trade as best I could
Lived my life just as I should

A Government person through and through
Super salaries, then I drew
Retirement filled in lots of time
Seasons changed and the sun did shine

Travelled the world by sea and air
Had no worries, free from care
Met many people in my time
Big and small, with all things fine

Age keeps travelling through the years
Along with all the ills and fears
A survivor though, through all that time
Times running out but I'm still fine

Knowledge though, I've lots to share
People though seem not to care
So I sit upon my chair and wait
No bag of bones, l tell you mate.

A Beach Walk

At Redhead Beach they walked along
She was humming a Christmas song
He, with shoes off, waded too
Among the sand and frothy goo

A bumper wave came and knocked his feet
Into the water, clothes and all, and fully beat
Mobile phone and cards and keys
In his pockets, if you please

To his feet, he struggled hard
But unable to lift all that lard
Help he needed, and so fast
From a person walking past

Home they hurried to change his gear
Glasses back upon his ear
A dryer out to dry his phone
In amongst his grunts and groan

The moral of this story then
If you should walk with lady friend
Let her walk the waters side
You stay where it's firm and wide.

Abreast with the Times

Abreast with the tea
But let all of us see
Red, black or white I ask thee
Enjoy what you see as long as it's tea

And with sugar and milk for me
Sit by the table, we'll see
The tea lady with the big chest
Will soon be along with the best

In with the sugar and spoon
There's more for you, if there's room
Heaps of coffee and cream
To go with you and your dream

Her actions are quite queer
Everyone can see clear
That the lady has tea on her mind
Including her chest, so I find

Maybe we'll see, with our cup of char
Each one should step up to the bar
Step out of the way if she comes your way
In case the cups fall off her tray

Sadly comes the time to say good bye
Adios, farewell which ever way you try
I'll raise my glass to the lass with the best
For I consider that she's stood the test.

A Bush Blowie

Of all the sights you don't want to see
A blow fly sitting here, next to me
The best thing then, for any man
Is grab the closest aerosol can

Those wings of his, in perfect motion
Shows by their noise, his location
A master of the air, he shows to be
Rivalled only by the honey bee

He's like a flash, when in the air
Flying about, not showing a care
His colours are bright, as he flies by
I cannot catch him, hard as I try

I'll open the door, give him a shove
Flapped at him with my oven glove
Outward and upward, quickly he goes
I close the door, trapping my toes.

A Camel Train

In the closing of the evening, just before it goes
    to sleep
A camel train is plodding, to a rest out in the deep
It has travelled many hours, making stops along
    the way
Before its destination and before the end of day

Many happy tourists have enjoyed a pleasant ride
While the camel driver ends his daily work with
    pride
He had handled camels and their heavy packs
Now he's looking forward to a night within his
    shack

There's been many days of travel, as he travels far
    and wide
Facing all the troubles of a camel driver guide
It's a long and lonely workload, as he sets the
    camels down
But he wouldn't change it for a job within the town

Just to feel the freedom of the life out in the bush
Against the life in cities with its hurry and its push
With the wind within the willows and a cuppa in
    the hand
Or to push the camels through the surf and through
    the sand.

A Cameo Judgement

He was thrown into the deep end
When asked to judge our verse
For it could have been our writing
Which would have been much worse

But this busy guy from Gloucester
A small hamlet in our north
Put down his pen and paper
And said "I'll give it all it's worth"

Then for days he sat and puzzled
Just to see whose coming first
It was easy in his judgement
To figure just who was worst

He read them all so carefully
Then he read them all again
He was careful with his judgement
To be sure who gets the fame

Stuck the poems upon a blackboard
Placed his hand upon his heart
Picked a missile from the table
And let fly, deftly, with a dart

Now the decision has been final
And the judge has made it clear
Who will be the winners
For computer-pals this year

Now this cameo of poetry
Written by the computer class
Resembles not the writings
Of the noted poets of the past.

A Cat's Dinner

There's a mouse upon my doorstep
He is looking for a home
Where he can be warm and sheltered
And then no more he'll roam

He scoots into the kitchen
To see what he can eat
He is such a tiny fellow
To make the pantry is a feat

But the hunger in his tummy
Makes a super mouse of him
He squeezes through the packets
For his body is so thin

And so this mighty rodent
His tummy now so full
Dashes from the pantry
Like a mighty raging bull

The cat now sees a movement
Not a raging bull he sees
But a pesky little rodent
Which will do nicely for his tea

The cat, in masterly fashion
Took a jump into the air
And landed on the rodent
To trap him, with great care

The mouse is now a captive
The cat, an easy winner
And if there were a menu
Guess what the cat will have for dinner.

A Cobbler's Tale

Went to the cobblers to see what he'd charge
Looked at my shoes, with head down he barged
New heels you need and your soles very thin
But the cost of the lot, you're in for a spin

"How long will it take" I asked of this guy
He tilted his head, looked up into the sky
Coughed one or twice, then looked straight at me
Depends on how much the demand will be

Repairs to heels and soles will be
A huge sixty dollars will be his fee
Two pairs of shoes, I think I could buy
With enough left over to buy me a pie

Went next day to pick up my shoes
Looked all over for one or two clues
No sign there was of my favourite pair
I looked at him hard and gave a big stare

Next to the garbage, he found them with glee
Sorry, he said, as he dropped down the fee
My shoes look great but needing a shine
I'll wait in his store, if there's a next time.

Across Australia

Across the eastern ranges
Across the western plain
It's heading ever westward
The Indian Pacific train

Four days across the waste lands
Where rain is seldom seen
The place of early explorers
We've seen where they have been

The scattered, lonely homesteads
Where the early settlers roam
Where tried and tested farmers
Settled and made their home

This land of rugged beauty
A land of heat and sun
The ever changing patterns
Where the 'roo and emu run

We see this from our window
From our air conditioned train
And wonder, from the distant
If only they had rain.

A Cry in the Dark

To the leaders of the nations
Hear my plea for Mother Earth
Stop pollution and destruction
Save this earth for all its worth

Days are getting hot and hotter
No one even seems to care
Just too busy making dollars
Not a care for cleaner air

Do you know the planets dying
For the lack of clean, fresh air
And the want of water flowing
Down a barren water course

Forest fires consuming nations
Killing fauna, and there's more
Floods and famine occur worldwide
Can be laid at your front door

I ask this question of world leaders
Does it matter who leads the band
When all that's left to rule over
Is a shattered, broken, wasted land.

A Day in the Life of a 95-year-old

A woke up early and fixed up my bed
Showered and shaved then off to be fed
Into the car, belted up with a clip
Left my home for a hospital trip

The sun was shining, a nip in the air
Twenty minutes should get me up there
But the cars on the road, a nightmare of mine
An hour later my eyes start to shine

The hospital in sight, glory to be
Sun shining down right upon me
But worse was to come, when I went to park
I'm not in the light but down in the dark

A spot I did find, on the basement floor
I thought to cancel, don't want any more
Walked to the lift, but what did I see
A sign, out of order, was looking at me

On to the stairs, two flights on the hop
I'm so angry and I getting quite hot
Finally a lift, but don't know to where
I'll have a seat and take in some air

Things look brighter, just one floor to go
The blood pressures working, going on low
Around the corner, things are familiar to me
This the place that I needed to be

Retracing my way, by lift and by stairs
Into my car with the thought of "who cares"
It's shopping now that I'm heading for
The shelves half empty when I reach the door

Now that I'm home, it's a cuppa for me
And a big bun to eat, as I watch TV
I've nodded to sleep and can't see the clock
I awoke in alarm, I should be up with the doc

Up to the doctors I travelled in haste
Leaving myself no time to waste
I sit in there and I think and wait
Just been told "the doctors running late"

Back home again, at last at rest
That's the thing that I do best
Tonight for dinner I'll cook a fry
On second thoughts it'll be a stir fry.

A Drive with God

Went for a visit, with doggie and wife
Out to the country, freedom from strife
To visit a parson, of whom I'd been told
Unannounced there, I felt rather bold

He welcomed us in, made us at home
Said that tomorrow we'd go for a roam
The day turned out a beautiful day
As we all prepared to get on our way

Into his van, squeezed a dozen of us
Ready to go, without any fuss
The road way windy, the driver unsure
Took the wrong road, of this I am sure

Around the bend, he took to the trees
Grasses and leaves wherever they please
Into reverse, and backward he sped
He'll not stop until we're all dead

Onto the road, He's off again
He's heading off somewhere, regardless of pain
The passengers white, and sweaty of hands
They have no idea of his driving plans

The parson in charge, he's gone up a gear
A look at the others is really of fear
One of the ladies lets out a scream
Waking me up from an unpleasant dream.

A Drover's Dream

I miss the call of the old "out back"
With the stockman riding down the track
His "bluey" hung at shoulder height
Ready to cling, if his horse should fright

A Hereford herd he's hustling along
Contenting himself with a cowboy song
Accompanied by the flies and dust
Riding on from dawn to dusk

A simple life, he's contented by
Pleasant thoughts, he just lets them fly
A week at home when this drive is done
To relax with wife and have some fun

Then back in the saddle, he's off again
Taking his herd to the cattle train
For shipment off to the city, bound
When he's left alone, with his faithful hound

Today the drover's life is past
Trucks come in, that move so fast
The rancher, eager for money flow
Keeps the truckies on the go

Life of the drovers, now in the past
Lost to the world, now moving fast
A page of history now seldom seen
Only, perhaps, in an "oldies" dream.

A Face at Rest

I saw a painting in the sky
It was there for all to spy
A head is what I saw, so true
On a background of vivid blue

I watched upon this pretty face
As she looked out into space
I wondered what the artist thought
And of the joy that it had brought

Of this picture in the sky
I often think, and wonder why
A sight like this is often seen
In the sky or in a dream

Fly on, my little princess cloud
You have left me feeling proud
Come visit me another day
If you pass along this way.

A Face in the Crowd

I saw a face amongst a crowd
A face so worn and yet so proud
I wonder what those lines would say
If I could read them, day by day

The hair is long, but turning grey
Well cared for, yet a few that stray
The eyes are bright, a shade of green
The prettiest eyes I've ever seen

The crowd moved on, her eyes met mine
I held her gaze for quite some time
Then she turned and moved away
Should I follow, or should I stay

Tomorrow then, she's there again
Attraction there, it seems so plain
I'll make a move to meet this lady
But oh, wait there, she's got a baby

Our paths have crossed, but I must wait
I'm not one to mess with fate
Then off she goes, this gentle one
And so for me, my race has run.

A Farmer's Life

I travel along the dusty road
My van contains a heavy load
The paddock's brown, through lack of rain
With the farmers facing drought again

The grass is sparse, the cattle lean
They know what lack of rain can mean
My heavy load is bales of hay
To help the farmers on their way

It's many months since rain did fall
Upon these lands, where the dingos call
And rabbits, in their maddened rush
Seek relief neath the stunted brush

The parrots, in their thousands, fly
Up in the deep, blue coloured sky
Seeking water, in their flight
Surveying everything in sight

This life is harsh, the farmers know
But when the clouds begin to show
And when the rains in torrents fall
Relieves the farmer's bankers call.

A Fisherman's Tale

A beautiful day and the sun was out
We're ready for fishing, no one about
Boat and trailer securely tied
Ready and right to do the ride

Down to the ramp, we quickly go
A change in the tide, it's on the flow
Boat released and into the water
We'll give these fish no quarter

A choppy sea, but we can take it
Rod and reel, we'll make it fit
A tinnie now and we'll settle down
"Damn", he cried, "left the bait in town"

We sailed on into the ocean
Another tinnie will ease the motion
A couple of hours, we're seeing double
Head for home and into trouble

Back on shore, we head for shops
No good buying nice pork chops
It's a fish shop now I'm looking for
And bought ourselves a neat score

Home we go, full of glee
Fish for all we'll have for tea
Into it chaps, no time to wait
When she comes in with our left bait.

A Fork in the Road

In this life we have many choices
Influenced by deeds and many voices
Roads we follow, as we travel on through
Choices we make, that will affect you

In early life, decisions are taken for us
Take it all steady, there's no need to rush
Parents and teachers, our mentors in life
Helping to mould us and kept out of strife

We head into adulthood; we're on our own
Heading along, and feeling full grown
The road we travel, with potholes and forked
We are to choose just which one is walked

Another fork in the road, it's marriage for us,
Soon there'll be children, no need to rush.
Babies soon arrive, brings their love
Time travels swiftly, they're no more a bub

Soon they've married and left with their load
It's time to download on another fork road.
Age and illness have forced this last move
Soon we'll be packed into another new groove.

Ageless

Age is the thing used every day
Whether at work, rest or at play
When with the young, it doesn't care
As for the older, it's time to beware

Age with the young, not even give air
We've ages ahead, why should we care
It's a word not in their vocabulary
Wait till they get to the age of poor me

The teens of this world, too busy, that's sure
They hardly have time to open the door
A bull at a gate, it's more of their style
I sit back and watch and ponder a while

In adulthood, I find, they're starting to think
Abusing the young that's causing a stink
This is the age of worry and care
With husband or wife, they have to share

When retirement comes, they've time to spare
Some can be seen on an old rocking chair
Others with hobbies, for which they make time
While in their life, the sun does still shine

We come to old age, where age really matters
Where often we find, lives are in tatters
Though life is near over, I look back in rage
And think of the times, I've wasted word age.

A Ghostly Night

In the still of the night, when all things seem right
The cat is out stalking, he looks for a bite
With the moon hanging low, and shadows abound
There's mice in the field, and the cat on the round

But all is not normal, a ghostly figure is seen
The cat with its fur up, its eyes have turned green
No sound to be heard, not even a breeze
Long shadows are seen, cast by the still trees

A shadow is seen, it's a ghost, I am sure
Making towards me, I head for the door
A groan, I hear, as I make my way in
Trip over the garbage, make quite a loud din

As I pick myself up, and dust myself down
A quick glance I give, as I'm moving around
Where did it go, is it inside or out
Can somebody help me, I give a weak shout

The night has progressed, I wake from my sleep
It's a dream that I've had, after counting the sheep
I'm covered in sweat and my throat is so dry
Don't know what's happened, perhaps I might die.

A Goat Tree

Goats to the west of me, goats to the east of me
Goats high in the old scrub tree
The herder is trying to round up his herd
The goats seem to think they're some kind of bird

Branches are bent with the weight of the flock
When the wind blows, the goat herd will rock
The farmer is worried, he wants to go home
If he gets his flock home no more will they roam

The sheep in the meadow, the cows in the corn
Goats in the scrub tree, the farmer not gone
He's waiting to see what the next move might be
Should he get a chain saw and cut down that tree.

A Golden Sunset

As the sun sinks slowly in the west
And birds have found their place of rest
The ocean waves roll gently by
As a breeze blows by, it gives a sigh

The painted clouds soon turn to red
Creatures have found their way to bed
Old sun has dropped his head from sight
The waves of sea give up their fight

Peace on earth, life settles down
A calm has settled over our town
The stars on high, twinkle bright
Things are seen through a moonlit night

Frogs are heard from a distant pool
Owls at flight in the evening cool
One settles down for a peaceful night
To wake, once more, to a morning bright.

A Hairy Tale

I visited a town named Ketchikan
Met a man with hair and whispers brown
A more rugged head could not be found
If you'd walked the length of town

A dog curled up and sound asleep
It's head upon this person's feet
A beautiful snap this man would make
My camera there the pic to take

I asked him if I could take it then
He shook his head, rubbed his chin
Pointed to his dog at his feet
A photo of him is yours to keep

I snapped the dog, then thanked the man
Started off, I waved my hand
He called me back and told a tale
Of how they treated this old male

With beard and hair both well grown out
Tourists then, from all about
Would snap and click and think it right
During day and even night

Continuing on, he said to me
You're the first this year, you see
To ask permission for the shot
So go ahead and take a pot

I thanked this man as I moved on
Glad I am my parent's son
For they had taught me the grace
To use within this human race.

A Happy New Year?

We hear the sirens screening as they head towards the fight
Where ash and smoke and fire turn daylight into night
There's many fearful men and women, pray, and wait to see
What plan of actions needed, be it wait or be it flee

There's no power, little water, but the fight must carry on
For through the smoke and debris we see a reddened sun
And the ash, that was a homestead, a ghost that's laid to rest
The men who fight these fires, the heroes of the best

Many thousand acres of this land we call our home
Has been eaten by this monster, as onward it must roam
Neither rivers nor the pilots, in the planes up in the sky
Can stop the advancing fires, but with them, it's do or die

The Government, in its wisdom, has called army into plan
And the navy used to evacuate, on the southern coastal land
With the heavy loss of buildings, and lives of many men
Can we stop this consuming fury, is it if, or is it when?

With the spirit of our fighters and the courage of the men
There will be "no give up", we will beat it in the end
If the Lord would send down water, in the shape of falling rain
It would help quench the fires and relieve our country's pain.

A He Ape

A wise old ape, you can see at a glance
Waiting a while before taking his chance
Surveying the field, while watching a male
Ensuring the fact that he doesn't fail

A noise from above and everything stops
While out from the bushes a little one hops
The group in turmoil, he shows the way
Young, uncaring as they leap and play

A young female soon catches his eye
He will follow, at least he will try
Now they're together, locked in embrace
He has made it, he won the race.

A is for Aunt

A is for Auntie, she wore the pants
She is the one who worked through the ranks
A hard-hearted woman she turned out to be
Often threatened with a dunk in the sea

She married a Scot, a brawny big lad
Marriage he said "wasn't so bad"
T'wasn't until she put in the screws
Then they started having some blues

A family of four, he didn't want more
Was enough to put food in the mouths of just four.
He turned to the drink, to lighten the load
As a salesman he spent time on the road.

At weddings and funerals came into his own
A belly of beer made him full grown
He'd stand with a glass and give a good toast
The words that he said was really no boast

"Here's to the health of your blood" he said
"Here's to the blood of your health" he read
"If you have good blood, you'll have good health" sip
"So here's to your bloody good health" then sit

The aunt looked daggers whenever he stood
Knowing the words would not make her look good
Her eyes diverted, she lowered her head
He'd get it tonight when she got him to bed.

AJ

AJ is lost, the headlines scream
A little boy lost, his mother's worst dream
Gone bush, in the scrub down Putty way
A call to police, they'll have a say

Police and rescuers are soon on the scene
Searching around places he's been
No signs have been seen on the first day
Oh, Lord help us, the parents pray

A night in the cold, how can he survive?
More searchers arrive, on motors they drive
Results are the same, no sightings are found
They check on the dams, perhaps he's drowned

Another night and a day, search is still on
But what is the hope for this little one?
An abduction is considered, still nothing is found
Searchers check tracks all over the ground

Things become desperate, search now full scale
What is the ending for this grim tale
Another night and a day, parents distraught
Where is our AJ, that is their thought

The fourth day begins, their hope, it is waning
Police carry on, as with their training
A "copter" on high soon sends out an order
Boy has been seen at a dam, drinking water.

A Kangaroo's Tale

The kangaroo hopped down the road
Upon his back was a heavy load
Leaving his mum and dad at home
Having to face his life alone

Hopped along, down into town
With many people standing around
He went into a grocer's shop
And kept the grocer on the hop

Helped himself to a lettuce heart
Snapped a celery stick in half
Jumped around with youthful joy
Like a wayward, naughty boy

The grocer finally forced him out
With lots of shouting all about
Up to the hills he quickly fled
Beneath his arm, a loaf of bread

Shocked and amazed, this little one
Had this day, a lot of fun
But on his own, he's left to roam
But then decides he's going home.

Mum and dad were quite shocked
As in, the wayward son had hopped
Welcomed him back into their home
And pledged that he, no more would roam.

A Koala

On top of the gum trees you'll see them there
Up in the treetop without a care
Curled up asleep, in the fork of a branch
Sleeping away, as if in a trance

Most of his day he lays in sleep
Opens his eyes when it's time to eat
No need to worry if the dingos yap
He's safely away as he takes a nap

Trees rock to the tune of a gentle breeze
When the winds blow it's likely to freeze
Leaves and branches weave and float
He stays warm in his thick, furry coat

Seldom he leaves his tree-top home
For food and water, no need to roam
His gum tree home provides it all
He's contented, rolled up in a ball.

A Leek

Went to the bathroom and what do I see
A leek 'neath the basin, as plain as can be
Is it a plumber, or green grocer I need?
It's sitting there, just like a green weed

Amongst the detergent and soaps it stands
The only thing there without any brands
What is it doing, what's it there for
If I look around, will I find more?

A prankster, no doubt, has put the thing there
The area around it would look very bare
A rat or a mouse would not eat a leek
I'll just sit around and have a wee peak

In comes a joker, with beady eyes bright
I speak to him, he trembles in fright
He's been caught in the act, shock on his face
Smartly he turns and runs out of the place.

A Leg Up

This left leg of mine, it's up in the air
It hurts and it's sore, as I sit on the chair
My leg, it is broken, or so I am told
Is that just because I'm getting old?

Went out shopping, with a friend, in a car
Came back quite soon, we didn't go far
Got out of the car, knocked my leg on the door
Just a small rap, it was nothing more

It ached and it throbbed, it will be better soon
Will just take a pill, lay down in the bedroom
Two weeks to the day, my son came on by
Took one look and to the hospital we fly

An x-ray was taken and three hours on
Your leg has been broken, said my bright son
With my foot in a boot, he drives me back home
Instructions I'm given, no more you will roam

So tonight I must look a great frightful sight
My boot and I, in the bed for the night
I've hobbled around for a fortnight or more
With a leg swollen and so extremely sore.

Alice and Friends

When Alice visited her great Wonderland
And played with her new friends on hand
The hare was there, with mad hatter as well
But who are the others, will someone please tell

A tea party arranged, for the new ones as well
We'll start whenever we hear the big bell
There're plates and saucers, for one and for all
We'll play some music, then dance round the hall

When the music is over and silence reserved
Tea and biscuits is next to be served
The visitors then, are allowed to go home
For poor Alice, no more will she roam.

All Bull

A bull goes into the china shop
The owner gives him a passing shot
The Bulls eyes showed a shade of red
Lowered his head and the owner fled

With head bent down and horns out-thrust
Charged a shelf which turned to dust
Around he turned, another barge
Before a full-on blaster charge

The bull, it seemed, was having fun
While the owner raced off to find a gun
On his return he let off a shot
But only blasted a China pot

The bull stood still, amid the route
The owner let out a mighty shout
Bull and owner, eye to eye
Decided then that one should die

With tail up high and head bent low
The eyes upon his annoying foe
Let out a roar and charged once more
Then headed for the exit door

The owner released a pent-up sigh
And eyed the bull, as it passed by
He knows it now, while his memory's hot
What a bull can do, in a china shop.

All Life Matters

Black lives matter, this is true
But remember, white lives matter too
So you go and protest, ignoring the rules
And act like a mob of irresponsible fools

You have ignored from the start
The laws that have been passed
For the safety of black and the white
For together we should be fighting this fight

While you're protesting, corona won't stop
So get out and fight it, non-stop
Do your part, stay alert and apart
Let's all be in it and smart

This virus is out there, waiting to breed
With no respect for colour or creed
Too many lives have been lost
And remember the cost

So black brothers and white
Get out there and fight
Together we'll fight it and be …
So give this virus the old one, two, three.

Alone

In the quiet home, she stands alone
Facial features, set as in stone
Mourning the loss of her husband dear
Now facing the virus, alone, with fear

Time, she finds, ticks slowly on
Wondering now of the world beyond
Her life today, by a twist of fate
The Lord took away her lifelong mate

This virus now, is the thing she fears
For she's been around many long years
Now home alone, with no one to share
She must be careful and go with care

Grocery shopping, she does by phone
Negating the need to leave her home
A phone call, from her son who lives away
Helps her through yet another day

When the sun comes up on a distant day
And the virus gone, to God we pray
She'll look again on a brighter time
When the world we know will be so fine.

A Love Tree

With arms close-wrapped around body
My heart just pumps, but rather soggy
What I feel, I can't fully explain
I just put up with aches and pain

It started off many years ago
When the winds would blow, to and fro
The arms grabbed on, to keep me safe
And anchor me in this here place

The years rolled on, the wind won't stop
It seems to keep me on the hop
I thank the arms for their devotion
And save me from the winds strong motion

We're here for keeps, I rather think
No point of kicking up a stink
The will of nature can be seen
On this pathetic, tragic scene.

A Magpie

A magpie, does it mean talking while eating?
Or is it a bird who lives and loves fighting?
Well it's either or both, the choice you must make
For the magpie won't give you a break

When August arrives it's the time for the pests
For the magpies start building their nests
With eggs in their nest, they're ready to fight
When they swoop from the sky, it's a terrible sight

They partner for life, these birds black and white
Be you short or tall, they feel it's their right
While they're guarding their nest
To dive bomb or swoop on the rest

We can't blame the birds, it's the way of the game
They'll fight till the end, showing no shame
Two months and they're gone, peace we'll regain
Until August appears once again.

A Merry Christmas

Christmas time has come again
For the children, it is plain
Fun and joy and Christmas cheer
For Mums and Dads a carton of beer

The children scream, in their delight
For Santa's made another flight
Bringing with him many toys
Smart phones for the girls and boys

Though the finances may be bent
Many dollars, no doubt, been spent
It's a one off thing each year
Joyous children we will hear

So to our friends in many lands
May your Christmas be as planned
We wish you all, joy and good cheer
So Merry Christmas and happy New Year.

A Morse Man's Dream

There's a Morse key standing in the hall
A sounder, leaning against the wall
They're the tools that we once sought
Sending Morse from port to port

No more the sound of click and clack
For the Morse has got the sack
But the memory still lingers on
With the men, most of them sadly gone

During wars, and in times of fear
Getting messages loud and clear
And in record time, for then
Who would think there'd be an end

S O S sent loud and clear
A birthday wish, to give good cheer
Meet the train, I arrive around six
Messages sent, it's been a mix

Now the only Morse I hear
Is in bed, the message clear
Morse still calls, it seems
In the realms of my dreams.

An Aussie Zoo

Come and see our koalas, bare
Among the gum trees standing there
Cuddly things for all to see
Living in the trees, so free

Or a platypus in secluded streams
He's the thing that's made of dreams
With his duckbill held up high
A flap of tail as he swims by

The Tasmanian devil, he'll raise your hair
Of all things in life, he'll not scare
The black and white, a perfect match
As he moves around in his own patch

The kangaroo and wallaby too
Will steal the hearts of each of you
And if a joey, you should see
Beside his mother, he will be

The dingo now, it's a different tale
Remember now, and do not fail
This native dog, you do not trust
Just watch him go, as he makes dust

The kookaburra, as he flies by
On you, he'll have his evil eye
And laugh at you, to see you duck
As he heads off, into his feed he'll tuck.

An Autumn Day

It was an early Autumn morning as the sun began
    to rise
Sending shafts of golden colour into a sky of azure blue
Soon the sun rays started chasing, the shadows of
    the night
Clearing out the valleys, turning night-light into day

As the sun reached higher, finding pockets still in dark
A golden glow of sunlight, showing all is right
A snow-white cloud was racing, straight across the
    scene
Appearing to be escaping from a gentle blowing
    breeze

The sun, in all its glory, fully now exposed
Demands to be acknowledged, by those around the
    skies
The wind, as though in acceptance, reduces speed
    to nil
While the distant stars of nighttime, fade away to sleep

The sun, now as the master, slides across the blue
Bringing warmth and sunlight, across the land below
The birds begin to chatter, animals on the move
Our world now in sunlight, a bright and happy scene.

Andrew Symons

"Howzat Out" quickly said the ump
Give him the ball, the batsman jump
Give him the bat, he's there to score
In the field it's catch and more

A run machine, he has become
Scoring figures by the ton
With the ball, he's lightning fast
As he's proven in the past

With painted lips and tasseled hair
A sight to frighten and to scare
In he runs, with ball afire
Caught in slips, decides the umpire

There's nothing on the cricket patch
That he can't beat or even match
In his cap of baggy green
He becomes a cricket machine

Warnie, Marsh and Symmo too
Family and friends are missing you
You'll remain in cricketing lore
Your names will live forevermore.

And the Rains Came

There had been drought for many years
And from the farmers many tears
As they battled through the seasons
While they tried to work out reasons

While the nature works out changes
Farmers push their cattle to the ranges
For their land is dry and dusty
And their water tanks are rusty

With the country dry and dying
We have flames of fires flying
Through the foothills and the ranges
Putting lives and homes in danger

Many months the fire rages
Haven't seen the likes in ages
Still the firemen battle bravely
As the country looks on gravely

Many thousand sheep and cattle
Lost their lives and lost their battle
To this large consuming flame
Man or nature, who's to blame?

When at last the fires beaten
And some million hectares eaten
There's the sound of thunder peeling
And the rain falls with a greeting

The skies have opened up above
With a chance, the rivers flood
And the paddocks turn to green
It will be a lovely dream.

An Early Winter

A beautiful morning, sun shining bright
The cold of winter is starting to bight
Snow on the mountains, sleet in the air
Forecasts saying the air is just fair

Off to the snow fields the snow skiers go
Hoping the mountain has meters of snow
Winter struck early with southerly blasts
More winds and snow is the weather forecast

It hit first the mountains, covered in snow
Then to the cities, see the wind blow
Folk in the country cover up tight
Trying to keep out the winter's cold bite

Sheep in the paddocks, tightly they pack
Keep the cold winds onto their back
Deep is the wool that covers the flock
Farmer is worried for his woolly flock

The dams, full of water, now turned to ice
Stock can't get at it, not even a mouse
A weak winter's sun tries to be bright
But cold winter's blow puts up a fight

The temperature drops to minus, we're told
That doesn't help when we're feeling so cold
One thing to remember, to keep out the pain
Summer awaits round the corner again.

An Elephant Story

While riding through the African wilds
I saw animals through the miles
Lions, tigers to name but a few
Hippos and rhinos in high numbers too

Gnus and monkeys, come to the fore
Many of these animals, I've seen before
But the sign on the road filled me with awe
I've not seen an elephant driving before

The sign I saw filled me with doubt
It makes me want to get out and shout
Elephants can read, and drive a car too
The marvel of science, to make it true

Poor old jumbo, can drive round the planes
I hope that he uses the correct motor lanes
Hoof signs does he give or uses the trunk
Can I see it, or am I still drunk?

A Neurotic Wife

The bedroom that we have in sight
Where husband and wife do not fight
The lines are drawn, as we can see
No arguments, are there to be

You stay your half, I'll stay in mine
Then everything will turn our fine
If it's love, by chance, you seek
You crossed that line just last week

I like to sit and preen myself
You know how fragile is my health
I lay and dream how life is fine
When I was wed, another time

But that broke up, because of He
He did not want to consider me
Then one night, away he went
When all my money, he had spent

So now, my love, just stay in line
Just give to me a little time
To do the things that I like best
While you stay on your half and rest.

An Obit for Me

To those of you, who have come to share
A lifetime spent in the sun and the air
It's the going down of another life
As I leave behind all my grief and strife

As a young child, life was so great
Spent most time with brother and mate
Nine long years I spent at school
Toe the line, was the golden rule

Friends I've had through school-time days
All predeceased, to spread out my ways
We'll meet again, in a far-off place
A place that we all, will finally face

A life of work, I am about to face
A telegram boy, I start, and at pace
Until at last, I'm a discontent
So off to Newcastle, my life went

Two years there, in the G.P.O.
Then off to Sydney, I'm bound to go
Sending Morse was the thing to do
Until it, too, died in '62.

In '52 I met Toni who became my bride
A red headed lass, left me with pride
In '53 a daughter so fair
Then '55 we had our pair

A change again in '64, I'm off to run elections
I sit awhile and ponder, look back in reflections
I've met the leaders of our lands
Whitlam, Fraser, Snedden and their bands

A divorce for me in '84, I was the one fell down
The children, both married, we were on our own
Soon I found a lady friend, no fun in living solo
With her we travelled globally, always on the go

In the year of '87 I'd had enough of toil
Took early retirement, my life was in turmoil
Flew to New Zealand on my first freedom day
No regrets on leaving, this I must say

I took a course in massage, to fill my vacant time
Also meditation, then everything was fine
Then it's travel, yes, travel, to see the world first hand
Ocean, sea and airways and travel where I can

US, Asia, Europe and places in between
Most of them we've seen
The seas and oceans also, we have sailed them too
Then across in Africa we have seen the natural zoo.

Poetry I started some twenty years ago
Now they're in the hundreds, I could put on show
Writing keeps me busy and keeps the brain alive
I do crosswords daily with this I do strive

Now in middle nineties, I go driving any day
In meetings and in outing, I still have my say
My walking's getting shaky but I do it anyway
I do the weekly shopping, but watch the pennies stay

I'm now living each day, as if it's my last
I've still many stories from back in the past
My memory is fine, it's the body not well
Will heaven take me, it's too hot in hell.

An Observation

Once upon a time, when the earth was round
Grass and trees grew all over the ground
Rivers ran from mountains to the sea
While birds and animals roamed so free

Then man came to planet earth
Raped the ground for all its worth
Polluted the rivers that ran to the sea
Our birds and animals no longer free

Volcanos, earthquakes and tsunamis came
Along with these came the disastrous rain
Towns and cities racked with pain
Because of mans greed and want of gain

Planet earth no longer serene
Cursed the place where man has been
Fighting back with nature's tools
To get the better of man, the fools.

Another Day

The sun goes down on another day
Night birds preparing to have their say
A golden glow in the west, we see
About to dip into the distant sea

A slight breeze blowing across the lands
Lovers talking, as they make their plans
Lights come on across the town
Exposing land, just turning brown

Babes wrapped up and in their bed
Meals prepared and the family fed
An owl is heard in the distant barn
Old men ready for their nightly yarn

The dog awaits his nightly rub
Old man's down at the local pub
Mum at home with the kids again
The Australian way, we see so plain

Sunlight dawns on a newborn day
Milkman out and is on his way
It seems a duplicate day in store
Just like the one we've had before.

Ants

A group of angry ants went out today
Determined for each to have its say
Our mother ant was first to talk
While others just stood around to gawk

A rousing speech, we all acclaim
While father ant just wanted fame
The baby ants were there in line
Making sure that they were fine

Another type, the termite kind
Got himself in quite a bind
Took himself off into the wood
As fast as he possibly could

It matters not, for one and all
For the termite man had a call
Killing ants, his aim in life
Be they be black, green or white.

ANZACS

We see them march on Anzac Day
The men and women, who went away
To fight our enemy, for one and all
And wept for those who had to fall

It's many years since World War One
With battles lost, but most were won
Returning soldiers then to the fore
With their thoughts of no more war

But lessons seemed not to be learned
For battle fields were soon returned
Our soldiers once more called to war
As they had, just years before

We see again, the spirit of the Anzac force
To battle on, with a new found course
Against a much advanced warfare
Of land and sea and in the air

So march on then, with heads held high
Like the airmen, who protect our sky
Though hearts are heavy and feet sore
March on and hope for no more war.

A Piston Tree

There's many a tree in Aussie land
Many I can call to hand
But a piston tree is new to me
As anyone here can see

I saw it out in the back of Bourke
Where many a thing, there lurk
Three Pistons in a growing tree
Four would be better than three

But the condition of the Pistons there
Is leaving the tree quite bare
To replace them in a pristine state
Is something I'd leave for my mate.

A spanner and wrench just would not work
The chain saw is a better lurk
But the tree itself is not looking great
The best I could hope, is faith.

Art, by Mother Nature

The dark of night has passed us by
A hint of light, not yet reached the sky
Another day we have today
Let's hope it's another magic day

I saw a painting on the sky
Unfortunately, it was just passing by
A painting on a sky of blue
Using nature's colours, so true

Clouds upon the horizon, sat
Some in white, others in black
A golden sunrise on the way
Touching clouds with a golden spray

As it rose from within the sea
Touching the clouds, a thing to see
Clouds of white turned into gold
A sight for all to behold

For just a sec. my world stood still
A spot in life, just so hard to fill
The sun rose high, the magic gone
But in my mind, the sight lingers on.

A Son's Speech

Everyone, I thank you for coming today
With cards and presents, you say
Celebrations for dad's 40th birthday
But first, I would like just to say

A few words to my "Abbu", my dad
For your support in life that I've had
Your love and help when I am down
A bright sunshine, when you're around

Our love, I want to point out to you
For all the things that you do
Just look at the folk gathered here
Waiting to give you a mighty cheer

It's your special day and I say
Happy 40th birthday today
From your family and friends, too
And know that we all love you.

A Spider's Tale

I saw an ant upon the wall
Afraid he's heading for a fall
For in the corner, I do spy
A spider watching, eye to eye

Ant soon sees his grave mistake
The spider does a double take
Then springs from his cobweb home
And for poor ant, no more he'll roam

The spider now, quite content
Energy, he finds, almost spent
Returns to home to sit and wait
For his wayward female mate

But as he waits, he hears a sound
Is it his mate homeward bound?
Or better still, a fly that's trapped
He'd better go and get it wrapped

With tummy full and eyes at rest
He doesn't need another pest
So into a ball he rolls and lays
To be contented for many days.

A Tale of a Whale

It happened at Eden, way down south
Washed up a whale with a great big mouth
Back on the beach it laid for many a day
Until the museum folk said, we'll make it pay

Moving the body, bone by bone
Into a new, temporary home
Partitioned off with fence and gate
So not to temp the word of fate

Then one night the villains came
Took the jaw out through the frame
Needing truck and jack to move
Thought that they "were in the groove"

Soon the police were on the scene
Looking where the jaw had been
Fingerprints were never found
But truck marks in the softened ground

News soon spread around the town
Information was quickly found
Police were on the trail, at last
Produced the culprits rather fast

The whale jaw then was back again
With it came a claim to fame
Soon to be on the museum floor
To bring visitors through the door.

At Sea

The caps, upon the oceans play
They often send off a little spray
As they, around the world, do flow
Sometimes rugged, sometimes slow

In the distance, one can see
A sailboat, on a tranquil sea
Up and down, it bob's and go
Aided by the gentle flow

Reflected on the ocean blue
Clouds above, sun shining through
A gentle breeze blowing by
Pleasant to the naked eye

The waves, now dance on high
A wind disturbed clouds in the sky
This brings on a heavy swell
Storms ahead, the sailors tell

Lightning flashes, thunders roar
Rain starts falling, more and more
Sailboat heads quickly for land
Wasn't like the day he planned

Tomorrow, though, is another day
He'll come out again to play
Upon these waters he calls home
Quite contented not to roam.

Attempted Escape

Went out for an early morning walk
And on the way, stopped for a talk
As we talked, I saw a sight
My eyes were glued, as if in fright

A tree, I saw, in walking mode
Walking down towards the road
It did not seem to notice us
Just carried on without a fuss

As we watched him make the pace
Away from the mud and water place
I thought how gentle he must be
But then he's just a humble tree

It seemed that he was needing rest
His pace, it seemed, was at his best
I returned to there the next morn
Only to find that he had gorn.

August

Cold is the bight of August's first blast
Up from the Snowy's, for days it will last
Sun is shining in a sky oh so blue
Not sending the warmth of a sun shining through

Trees bent and waving, showing displeasure
Standing there in all kinds of weather
Light clouds are seen hurrying past
Chased by the winds, they move very fast

Few birds are seen in this type of weather
Tucked up somewhere, with heads in their feathers
Even the owl, tucked up in his home
Knows not the time for his daily roam

A month and a day it's likely to last
That's what it's done, this month in the past
We've seen it happen year after year
We're wrapped up and warm, in a house full of cheer.

Ausom v Awesome

We've heard of a mob in the south
I won't say they have a mighty big mouth
But Ausom they are, a rather large club
Yet we are the ones from Newcastle hub

We spell awesome a much different way
And awesome are we, and we'll make you pay
Our entries are in, awaiting the votes
We make the most of our little jokes

With poetry and writing, we'll give it a go
Then when it's all over we'll give you a blow
Photography too, we'll give it a shot
Our cameras, I'm sure, are running quite hot

In October we'll see, at the end of the race
If you Ausom's enough to keep up the pace
Eyes to the shutters, hands to the pen
Is Newcastle club the champions again?

Australia Day

Australia Day, sing loud and clear
For we've travelled through another year
Advance Australia in song and praise
As we advance to another phase

The flag is flown through city and town
Over pastures green and country brown
It matters not, for we are one
As we forge on and our songs are sung

Our beaches shine in our summer heat
As we prance about on tender feet
And watch the waves break on the beach
Where lifeguards watch and also teach

The kangaroo and wallaby call
Among the trees, so gaunt and tall
And the muted call of the turtle dove
Reminds us all of this land we love

Where summer heats reach forty plus
And fires burn with heated lust
Yet winter times it's cold and bleak
Where six degrees would be the peak

Our coat of arms, and flag so tall
And one and all, we must recall
The wars that made this country great
And gelled us all as mate for mate

With singlets, shorts and airy thongs
We're Aussies one, with Aussie bonds
So raise your glasses, and let us pray
As we celebrate our Australia Day.

A Walk in the Park

Spring into Japan for a walk in the park
Or perhaps you'd go, just for a lark
Colours perfect, scenery Devine
Seems to be etched straight out of time

Perfume of flowers, adored and appeals
Into their bottles and quickly they're sealed
Off to the markets, worldly they're sold
Into the shops, for young and for old

The colours of Japan, a sight to behold
Whether in summer or winter's cold
My Fuji a picture in its winter gown
The bullet train as it runs through town

Geisha girls, with their painted faces
Can be seen in many towns and places
Colours and lights keep cities bright
Mix with the beauty of this countries sight.

A Welcome to Winter

Summer finally over, trees standing bare
Days are getting shorter, rain is in the air
Winter flowers peeping through a heavy ground
Grasses in the paddocks, turning now to brown

Calling of the fledglings, as they have left the nest
Fallow grounds upended, as they are left at rest
Icy gales start blowing, dusting tops and peaks
Snowfalls in the mountains, continue on for weeks

Antarctic winds are blowing, across a turbulent sea
Blowing, ever blowing, as strong as it can be
To carry forth the elements, to make a winter freeze
Painting white the landscape and the tallest trees

Winter brings the changes, brings the playing grounds
For those who love the skiing, in many country towns
Those who hate the winter, head north for winter sun
Leaving those who love it, to have their winter fun

For weeks we battle onward, to face the winter blast
Rugged up, we wait patiently, till we see it leave at last
Winter finally over, we see the Spring once more
With spring now in our footsteps, winters gone, for sure.

A Whale of a Tale

From the south they come, to breed in the north
Come in their thousands, in Autumn each year
Once they were hunted, today they swim free
Breach as they pass, flip tail without fear

Gone are the years they were killed for their fats
They're King of the waters, they weigh a good ton
They swim in dozens or even in pairs
A breech and a dive, while they're having fun

When they've been in the north, babies are born
Then they turn to the south, again homeward bound
Mothers are seen, with their infants in tow
Following the herd and directed by sound

They stay in the south for the rest of the year
Feeding on krill from the ocean so deep
When Autumn returns the migration begins
Beaching and diving, there's no time to sleep.

A Wishing Well

Well, well. I always wanted a wishing well
Think of all the things that it could tell
In fact, the wishing well, it is a must
You could end up owning a full size bust

Be careful what you wish for
Don't be greedy, don't ask for more
Some would wish for things adored
While others think it's just a fraud

How deep the well, I do not know
There's nothing there for you to show
But if you're tempted to the well
The burden is for you to tell.

A Worldly Thought

Today I walked the empty streets
With just the policemen on their beats
No bus, no car, no people seen
Could be a moon type movie scene

But then I see a mongrel dog
Heading out from behind the log
An eerie feeling settles over me
Is this what life is yet to be

A police car creeping down the road
On his shoulders, a heavy load
Keeping this city locked down tight
To help us win this vital fight

A runner then, comes upon the scene
His daily run, is where he's been
No mask upon his sweaty face
As he heads home towards his base

The sun shines bright and clears the fog
There's no sign of the wayward dog
The police cars gone, gloom remains
Adds more strength to our aches and pains

A sorrier world, I'm yet to see
No more do we have a pristine sea
Rivers, creeks and waterways
Spewing out trash to ocean bays

How much more can our world take
Flood and fires left in its wake
Alpha, Beta and Delta too
What is left that our world can do?

A Zoo Visit

I took a walk around the grounds of the Western
    Plains Zoo
Among the trees and grasses and where the orchids grew
I put my hanky on a rock like Hercule Perot would throw
Before I sat myself where moss and lichens grow

I just sat upon that rock and watched the world go by
Up in the trees, a monkey, I could catch him if I try
Then a rustle in the grass caused quite a big surprise
For the rock that I sit upon moved slowly as it tries

Where my mobile seat is going, I really do not know
The only thing for certain, it will move me very slow
It really does surprise me that a rock can move at all
The only thing of comfort, it won't hurt me if I fall

This strange and mobile rock, perhaps it comes
    from Mars
What other explanation for a rock that moves like cars
It's heading for some branches, I guess I'd better duck
Or I could end up like a great big lump of muck

My eyesight isn't perfect, is that the guide I saw
It's just a friendly fellow, wants to show me to the door
My entry fee is valid, Mr Magoo was at the gate
I'll have to go and face him and learn about my fate

I was sitting pretty, on my hanky on the rock
Taking in the beauty, until someone turned the lock
Now they left me in the traffic, hanky in my fist
The rock from distance Mars is the only thing I'll miss.

Baby Show

We were out walking, the morning so bright
Then stopped for a coffee, all was so quiet
She asked me to go to a small baby show
But when we got there, I'm in for a blow

Guess who was told, "You're the judge for today"
There's twenty young brats, what can I say
The first one I saw, red hair and blue eyes
Hair tied up with a heap of blue ties

The next one was brown, of Asian decent
A nice looking babe, if it's nose wasn't bent
Mums gather round, smiles on their face
Each one wanting their child in first place

I'm confused as I go, can't remember the first
Only half through, that is the worst
Of all the ones that I've already passed
What will I remember when I come to the last

Sun no longer shining, black clouds overhead
I look at the babies, they all look well fed
A flash of lightning, then thunder so plain
A dash for cover as down comes the rain

Surprise and relief for the judge of the day
No more judging, whatever the pay
The show is deferred, to a date to be found
But their previous judge, nowhere to be found.

Bank Holiday

It's seven o'clock, the world is up
Gulping coffee from a cup
Gobbling down a slice of toast
While glancing at the Morning Post

Donning shorts and canvas shoes
Hurry, there's no time to lose
Where on earth's that other lace
Must have lost it in the race

Tearing to and from the car
Hurry, or we won't get far
Throwing stuff into the back
Spade and towel and plastic Mac

Got the sandwiches and the mugs
Vacuum flask and travel rug
Right! All set? Then off we go
Where are we going? Don't you know

To the sea, to swim and play
And find somewhere for us to stay
In a house out on the Bay
Because today is bank holiday.

Barney the Bull

Barney, the bull, was feeling great
As he crashed through the farmer's gate
Then headed off, on a route he made
To visit with his jersey maid

He made pace, as best he could
Jumping over the fallen wood
For he knew that the farmer boss
Would be after him with his dog, Moss

In the foreground he could see
The maid, waiting beneath the tree
But in the distance he could hear
A noise, which filled him with great fear

The stock whip cracked, the hound-dog bayed
He feared his love tryst may soon fade
But on he went, with head held high
The question is, will I live or die?

He rushes on, his love in sight
He is ready for a real big fight
But the farmer, with his dog, moss
Is there to show just who is boss

With head hung low, he heads for home
They'll make sure he'll no more roam
Sending him off to the abattoir
Alas for Barney, no more amour.

Battered Fish

I saw a sign upon the wall
As I was walking through the mall
It's big and bold for all to see
Relates to things from within the sea

Battered fish, the sigh had read
Imagine that, and before they're dead
A mallet then, it must have been
For there was nothing else I'd seen

I stood, amazed, to think that they
Would attack fish and make them pay
Battered here and battered there
Poor old fish, I'd like to spare

A bag of prawns will have to do
With them I'll make a curry stew
And leave the battered fish at bay
There you go, I've had my say.

Battle Cry

From Australia they came, with blood in their eye
Ready to fight yet willing to die
Young Aussie men with pride and with worth
To battle the Japs, who invade from the north

In Rabaul they battled, till finally beaten
Prisoners of war, they finally became
A thousand prisoners and Japanese crew
All packed on to the Montevideo Maru

Off to Hainan, they travelled at night
Watching for ships, as they travelled in fright
Sturgeon, the sub, sent a torpedo away
Down went the ship, in a deathly spray

Eighty long years it lay there at rest
At the bottom of the ocean, the men of the best
One thousand Aussies, no more will they roam
But peace at last, for the loved ones at home

At the War Memorial, their names flashing bright
With Honour and courage, for all there to sight
The horrors of war and the lives of our men
May we all say, Lest We Forget, amen.

Beauty

Beauty comes in many ways
Through the nights or through the days
Moonlight with its silvery glow
Or flowers when in glory, show

The waterfalls in river's flow
Salmon when they jump, on show
Reflections on a forest lake
An apple there for you to take

Flowers in the gardens, green
A peacock as he sits and preen
An eagle, as he floats on high
All below a faultless sky

Nature, as it's bound to show
Pictures in the white of snow
The landscapes of a barren land
Pictures painted, but not by hand

Ships upon the oceans crest
Dolphins, as they too are blessed
Drifting off, across the blue
All these things, she gives to you.

Bee-ware

Is it a fairy, or is it a bee
Trying to tempt me with coffee, I see
The wings are busy as she flies on by
I can't stop laughing, as much as I try

"You know you want this" it's there to see
Perhaps she thinks, this is for me
The look of the body, not pretty at all
Just look at the legs, she's ready to fall

Coffee fairy, you're really a freak
Is that a nose, or is it a beak?
The pleats of the skirt, do nothing for me
A quick look at you and I'm wanting to flee

But honey, my friend, when all's said and done
Nothing's beyond me, I'm just out for fun
I'll have me a coffee, with milk, if you please
With scotch finger biscuit, just as you leave.

Being Australian

Across the oceans, the ships had come
Loaded with convicts and gallons of rum
The travel was long, the seas were rough
The ships and men were all so tough

For months they sailed, sick with pain
Fighting the seas, the wind and rain
Until at last the land was seen
With trees and grasses, all so green

The convicts soon, were put to toil
Building homes and working the soil
Until at last, as free men they roam
To build this country, and their home

The years pass on, generations change
Across the mountains, settlers range
Exploring more, this ancient land
To build into this, a nation grand

Our forefathers, our men of past
Have built this country, first and last
Created cities and cleared the land
Today we see all this, firsthand

A nation now and proud to be
Built by stock that came by sea
A greater place could not be found
I'm going to stay Australia bound.

Birdbrain

Over in Holland the police are rough
Caught a little bird doing things tough
He'd joined a gang of criminal men
Soon he's chased by the policemen

A robbery had then taken place
Police in force, had used their mace
The police had said, they had the word
Arrested all, including the bird

Journalists soon heard the story
Interviewed bird in all its glory
In a cell with bread and water
Cared for by the warden's daughter

Birds identity unrevealed in case
So a black mask across its face
But the full and final fact
It's really just a bird brain act.

Birds

You've heard about the movie, Birds
With Hitchcock and his famous words
I went along, my friend and I
Got so scared, I thought I'd die

We walked home, in the pitch-dark night
Every move and noise caused fright
The Moon too, seemed to be in hiding
As we passed by the railway siding

At that time we were in our teens
Not prepared for the world, it seems
But battle on, we're homeward bound
Dutch courage then is all we've found

Home at last, a toilet stop
A "dunny" out in the garden top
Upon the roof, a great big bang
From the rafters, I did hang

Into the house, a shower taken
The bones are weak, the body shaken
In future when Hitchcock is on
You won't find me; I'm long time gone.

Birds, Birds, Birds

From our back door, we see birds galore
Corellas we see, two hundred or more
Fighting, screeching and dancing at play
But leaving a mess, as they fly away

Next day we could see two dozen at least
Galahs on the lawn, having a feast
Contented are they, till they're chased away
By the crows that come late in the day

Plovers have nested, they call this place home
Each year they arrive, this is their zone
Last year they had four, all of them killed
As far as they go, don't have many skills

This year they're back, with three in the nest
A local tom cat, took two, he's a pest
Now there's one little chick, with parents around
In their protection, he races all over the ground

There's also the common, the starling and sparrow
They're quite contented to feed from the barrow
The King parrot at times, comes onto the scene
But they are so timid and it's seldom they're seen

It's pleasant to watch, from the window or door
While I keep watching, who knows what's in store
As the seasons change, so do the birds
But whatever the season, I'll find the words.

Birdwatcher

A birdwatcher from way out west
Came to put this hobby to the test
Of watching birds up in a tree
Saw a falcon clear as can be

The eyes stuck out at what was there
It was more than he could bear
A falcon in the tree, for sure
But not the one he's looking for

There's not a feather to be seen
In this tree so dark and green
But a falcon, a motor car
With its doors left all ajar

With binoculars down to rest the eyes
Took out a hanky, then he cries
The falcon, a bird so rare
The world about, it's just not fair.

B is for Beauty

B is for beauty; it's only skin deep
Or that is the version they want you to keep
But beauty is seen wherever you look
Whether the earth or in a still brook

Deep in the forest are the beautiful birds
Gazelles in Africa in their big herds
Even the elephant, majestic and tall
And look at the sight of Victoria falls

The sight of the sunrise, out in the east
Or viewing the moon, that's hard to beat
The colours of rainbows, high in the sky
And the big old emu, too heavy to fly

Wings of the butterfly, displayed with their grace
The cheetah in motion, as she runs her race
A green frog in the pool, loved by her mate
Even the children, who swing on my gate

As I go through life, it's beauty I see
Whether on land, or natures deep sea
Beauty abounds, wherever I look
I write it all down in my life's book.

Black Cat

I overlook a neighbour's flat
In her window sits a black cat
I see him sitting there each morn
By midday though, he's up and gone

Her house cat is black and white
But of her cat I have no sight
Just this one upon the pane
Is it right, or am I insane

Quickly then my cameras out
Take a snap, then give a shout
Through my lens, it's there to see
A black cat where it shouldn't be

A reflection then it's got to be
From a shrub or some small tree
But to me it's very plain
A black cat on a windowpane.

Bluey

I'll tell you folk a story, of a fella I once knew
Tied a billy to the tail of a monster kangaroo
Then released it again, you shoulda seen the dust
Wouldn't stop, I'd wonder, till he hit the distant
    brush

He took a herd of cattle, just he and his two dogs
Spent his nights at slumber between two darkened logs
Started off with thirty, and arrived with forty-two
He was a hefty redhead, we called this fella Blue

I remember many years ago, he was just a little lad
Got himself into all pranks, though he wasn't really
    bad
Just a sense of humour, from a warped unsettled mind
When strange things happened, it was him they
    always find

I saw him ride an emu, out on the edge of town
The emu won the battle, and old bluey hit the ground
The emu took a gander, turned, and headed for home
All we heard from bluey, was a long, extended groan

Took a camel train up north, was The Alice in his sight
In the footsteps of the great, the Afghani and their
    fight
Many days up in the saddle, as the column
    travelled on
Reached his destination at the setting of the sun

He was known to tell a story, be it false or be it true
When he flew a fighter with a full Australian crew
Yet the annals of his wartime, not a mention is it there
Still this mans a hero and a fighter without fear

Many years have passed, since I saw old Bluey last
There are changes, sad to say, he is ageing rather fast
No more will he be chasing the elusive silver dollar
For around his neck he wears a pastor's collar

He now has time and effort and ability to give
Asked for forgiveness and a better life to live
Heads now into life with prayer book in his hand
Pleased with his life and in Gods massive band.

Bob, My Friend

I rang to have a natter to my cousin and my friend
To be told my cobber had reached his journey's end
With heavy heart, I remembered, the days when
    we were boys
When we would play together, in the dust and with
    our toys

Soon our lives had altered, we went our separate ways
Bob became an architect, from Snowy Mountain days
His paint brush became his ruler, the master of his life
Left the Snowy Mountains and took himself a wife

We met again in the seventies, we're both "The
    Centre" bound
He's off to paint The Olga's and Alice Springs, the
    town
This trip he made to Alice, commenced his road to
    fame
Today the name of Lovett, has become a household
    name

The world has been his "oyster" 'He's travelled far
    and wide
And many are the paintings that he had shown,
    with pride
The man from Snowy River, racing through the trees
And Clancy of the overflow were really just a breeze

Now The Master's called him, he needs an artist there
To paint the morning sunrise, and setting sun, with care
When I wake at morning, and look into the sky
I'll see a beautiful sunrise, with a tear within my eye.

Bring Me Back

Bring me back, when I flash, wobble or beep
For my stone heart, you should all weep
For I stand here each day and I wish
That my body would be turned into flesh

The world has meant so much to me
And my baby that I hold here in glee
Our hearts beat together as one
As we stand here together in sun

I fought for my son to be free
But he's now stuck here with me
We honour this world where we live
But just how much more do we give

Our ties to the earth are so strong
I don't think we've done anything wrong
We ask you, now from the deep
Bring me back, when I flash, wobble or beep.

Bull Frog Fight

Two bull frogs sat on a grassy stem
Other frogs just sat watching them
Inch by inch they moved together
Then from the sky, dropped a feather

If as a sign, they attacked each other
Into the pool they fell together
A croak from here, a croak from there
They both came up to get some air

Back under water the fighters went
Murky waters was all they sent
Round and round the contestants fought
Being the winner, is what they sought

A calm settled over the tranquil pool
No breezes blowing, pool quite cool
Slowly then, one head appeared
The other lay dead, or so it's feared.

Bushrangers

Many stories have been told
Around our great Aussie towns
Fables of the Kelly gang
And how they made their pounds

There's Clancy of the Overflow
And the man from Ironbark
Thunderbolt, the outlaw
Who loved a moonlight lark.

Let's not forget the Irish lad
Our wild colonial boy
He'd kept the coppers on the run
While robbing was his ploy

There's many past and present
Who take money of all kinds,
Insurances and bankers
Are the ones that came to mind.

But then there's many others
Who put Ned Kelly's fame to shame.
They are our politicians
Who take our money as fair game.

Cadburys

For a hundred years, in Hobart town
Cadburys chocolate have been around
With their goodies wrapped in usual blue
Loved by all, that are real Aussie true

I remember the time, long, long ago
When dad had no job, money was slow
I'd go to the store, just like today
Bought a Cadbury, and a penny I'd pay

Years have moved on, flavour still there
Many varieties for those who do care
Freddo a favourite with children today
Picnic and roses for parents, they say

Whatever your choice, there's one there for you
If you're not happy with one, you could always
    have two
There's one thing for certain, this I am sure
Cadbury will be around for a hundred years more.

Camel Driver

From Afghanistan they came, camels and all
Hardy bush men, the strong and the tall
To carry the produce, from out in the west
Doing the job that they knew best

Many years on, they carried the load
All the way on until the railroad
Camels let loose to fend at their best
Thousands now roam out in the west

The railway now from south to the north
Carries the cargos that they once bought
Passengers too, are carried by train
The train lovingly christened the Ghan

From Adelaide to Alice they move overnight
Chugging along in the dark and the light
At Alice Springs they visit the town
Before boarding the Ghan, Darwin bound.

Caught

Been out on the town, I had a bad night
Was up and about, no one was in sight
Garden out front needed watering, I told
So off I go, not bright nor so bold

A neighbour caught sight, some distance away
She must have thought I was ready for play
Up into the shadows, she cautiously came
To see, I think, if I was playing some game

As she got closer things even got worse
She'd left her glasses at home in her purse
The looks from her were daggers for me
I couldn't help what she thought she could see.

Centuries

A hundred years ago, or so I'm told
Spanish flu put the world on hold
Thousands died, and many more
Than died in the trenches of the Great War

One hundred years, it's on again
The corona flu, along it came
Thousands died, of this I'm sure
Taking the sick, the old, the poor

In one hundred years, what will we see
Another flu, death and disease?
Will the world be ready with a cure?
But I won't be around, of this I'm sure.

Chicken Dinner

Chickens to the left of me, chickens all around
Healthy chickens all, in yellow, white and brown
Into this world of dinners, they have a lot to learn
Could he have one for dinner, or his head he'd
    have to turn

Keep the chickens happy, his lesson for the day
Even if he hurts one, I'm sure he'll have to pay
Not one of them is worried, don't know the word
    of fear
Do not get anxious, just watch the pussy's ear

In this world of wonder, I wonder what you'll do
Never trust the pussy, he'll make a chicken stew
Now you have the message, remember what I say
Eyes upon the pussy, and live another day

Reclining on this pussy is not the thing to do
He could change his colours, end up eating you
Options are your choices, use them at your ease
Remember that pussy won't listen to your pleas

Pussy looks so harmless, treating you OK
Until it's time for dinner, then he may make you pay
So listen, little chickies, brothers, sisters all
Set yourselves a target, before you have a fall.

Chimp Chump

I'm up a tree, is this all that life's to be
Won't someone come and sit with me
I keep a lookout for a friendly face
Can't seem to find one in this place

The forest's dark, there's trees to climb
No one seems to have the time
To come and climb some trees with me
And be as free as you can be

Here I'll sit, in awe and wonder
As if in life, a clap of thunder
Should wake me from my daily woes
To set me up with twinkle toes.

Christmas '21

Christmas time has come again
Comes through snow, dry or rain
With the covid delta here
Will he come with his good cheer

Though the year has been severe
He'll be here, we do not fear
With his reindeer masked up to
To stop the covid, not the flu

Santa, with his mask of red
Won't stop him from being fed
Or the sip or two he takes
Hang on there, has his sled got breaks

Poor old Santa and his crew
They've been around a year or two
Knows the ropes, of this I'm sure
He'll have toys forever more

So mums and dads, get out the rum
There's still time for lots of fun
Let your hair down, let things flow
He'll squeeze through the banks of snow

Hang the socks, get out the tree
Santa comes to you and me
Set the table, bring out the beer
Merry Christmas and happy new year.

Christmas '22

It's Christmas time in another year
Santa's coming with loads of cheer
Sleigh all loaded, reindeer's fed
An early night, we're all for bed

The reindeers up, with eyes aglow
Though two feet deep in winter snow
Come on Santa, it's time to go
Let's get moving, now don't be slow

Kids the world over just waiting for you
Hop into the sleigh, your helpers too
Loaded with goodies for girls and boys
An occasional bottle is parents' toys

Up into the sky, and off we go
We have a tailwind, so let it blow
Down below, in the dark of night
Children wait for morning light

The drops are made, with love and joy
Lovely gifts left for girl and boy
An empty sleigh and off we go
Back to our home, with ice and snow.

Christmas Do

We were at the Christmas party
And the food was passed around
When she opened up her mixture
With no spoon to be found

But Di, from her Pandora box
A spoon was quickly found
The one who had forgotten hers
Soon was eating food so sound

Though the lunch is almost over
But the story's not at end
She sat erect and stated
I thank you, my friend

There's no return of spoons yet
She sat and looked contented
I said then, quite so low
A body search may be attempted

A sudden look of terror appeared upon her face
Then, as if by magic, the missing spoons appeared
I grabbed the spoons and hid them
Like magic, they just disappeared.

Christmas is Coming

Christmas is coming, there's work to be done
Santa is working, his aim is for fun
With sleigh newly painted, new decor and all
Even the reindeer are waiting on call

There's an IPad for Sarah, a bike for our Paul
James will be happy with bat and new ball
The sleigh will be loaded with things for the Dad
Mums not forgotten, she'll be so glad

The weather is colder, it's starting to snow
Just look at the peaks, they're starting to grow
The reindeer are frisky, biding their time
This time of year they're ready to shine

Work carries on with the toy making crew
Painting is done with the red, white and blue
Packed into parcels, packets and box
Matching up with Santa's white locks

Children are sleeping away in their bed
Hardly a whisper, from what I've heard said
Dreaming away of where the snow falls
Patiently waiting for Santa's first calls

Up in Lapland, where Santa Claus dwells
Packing the sleigh and watching it swell
Rudolf and friends now harnessed and set
Off to the South where Santa is met.

A Merry Christmas and a happy New Year
May you have fun and a lot of good cheer
Open your presents, that you hold so dear
Be good, be happy, we'll see you next year.

Christmas Wishes

Jingle bells, jingle bells, it that Santa I hear
Is it really the end of yet another year
The years come around quicker, I fear
But Christmas it is, I tell you, my dear

The shops are in bloom, like a beautiful flower
With puddings and cakes, and lit up like a tower
The children are singing their Chrissie songs
And trying to repair their yearly wrongs

With Rudolph and gang, locked into their gear
They're leaving their home, not even a tear
For Aussie's the place they want to be
The smiles on kid's faces, they want to see

Sleigh loaded with goodies, releases the brake
For Aussie before nightfall, they want to make
No if's or no but's, they're up in the sky
To deliver their load, it's do or it's die

For Santa, he knows, just who have been good
With presents for all, just under his hood
To please mother and dad, a carton of beer
And the rest of the world, he wishes good cheer.

C is for Choppers

C is for choppers, that's teeth to you
The things we use when we chew
But over the years they start to wear
And that's when they make you swear

You brush and scrub for many years
They even drive you to hurtful tears
And when the dentist looks inside
There's really no way for you to hide

So off to the dentist, you slowly go
A man you treat as a painful foe
Open wide, is the call you get
As you sit in the chair and fret

With needle in and jaw set wide
You try to show your braver side
But blood and pain is not your game
And when it's over you're wracked with shame.

Clocked

The clock upon the kitchen wall tells me more than time
Tells me what the weather is and when the sun will shine
When I look upon the dial, it seems to wink at me
I wonder if it's knowledge is more than I can see

It's face it bright and shiny, with hands as black as coal
The thing that sits upon the clock looks like a tiny mole
I plugged it in and let it go, it seemed to have a glow
Then the hands start moving, around the dial they go

The hands of time are working, and working very fast
I'll have to get a move on or I'll be coming last
The time has come to midday, the hands now look like one
I'll leave the time behind me and have a little fun

Many years have passed, the clocks still on the wall
Keeps me up with weather and when the snow may fall
Yet one of us is slowing, it still looks good to me
The answer is so easy, I'm slowing up, you see

I've no need to wait and worry and wonder about time
The clock upon the kitchen wall is really doing fine
I'll sit and read another book and let the hands go round
Dictated by the hands of time, I'll end up underground.

Cloe

"My baby is missing", came the mournful cry
As she looked to heaven, in a clear blue sky
Police were called and a search is underway
Please find our little baby, for this we do pray

The searchers came from far and near
All anxious and filled with searchers fear
That little Cloe was lost out in the bush
As night approached, they gave an extra push

The search continued, into the dark of night
Weary searchers hurried, looking for some sight
Tired men and women, almost now in tears
Carried on regardless, to beat their rising fears

The sleeping bag is missing, this was noticed soon
Could she have been abducted, beneath the moon
A week of fruitless searching, nothing to be found.
Police have now decided to turn this search around

They search the home and area, where the family play
Hoping for a clue, to help them on their way
A million dollars offered for information help
To solve the mystery that the little girls been dealt

To the shattered family, who have put their life on hold
Until the very moment they welcome Cloe into the fold
May the police and searchers, working hand in glove
Have the help and guidance, from the Lord above!

Cloe is Found

Cloe is missing from family and home
Taken at night where dark shadows roam
Lost to the world, is how it must seem
To the family at home, like a bad dream

Volunteers and police, to the rescue they came
Searching the brush, streets and the lane
Days turned into weeks, still nothing was seen
No traces at all where Cloe had been

The home was searched, yet there were fears
Her family heartbroken and holding back tears
Posters were planted all around town
No news was getting everyone down

Early one morning, in Carnarvon town
Policemen were convinced she could be found
Entered a home and to their surprise
Cloe was to greet them with big open eyes

She's been found, she's been found, out goes the cries
Tears soon appeared in so many eyes
The hearts of the parents were beating again
Leaving behind all the aches and the pain

With the family whole and together once more
Their good news has travelled from shore to shore
The police, in hundreds, are covered in glory
Bringing to close an extraordinary story.

Cloud

When I was on this earth of ours
I worked at many things
I joined the senior's computer pals
T'was there I got my wings

Time went by, I got the call
Went up there above
Learned the ropes best I could
Then I got the shove

Was put upon a nice white cloud
When first I started here
Do you know the things I saw?
I'll tell you then, my dear

The stuff that people send to cloud
It would really make you smile
They tell me all their secrets
And I keep it in a file

I know what politicians do
And how they spend their time
Who they even spend it with
And how they save a dime

There're others too, they're unaware
They send stuff to me to keep
If they knew what I know
I'm sure that they would weep

And so, my friends, I have advice
If you want to act out feral
When you decide to use the cloud
Just send it at your peril.

Clouds

I saw a cloud just floating by
Painting a picture in the sky
With gentle shades of grey and white
As graceful as a bird in flight

A wind came by and changed the sight
The wind and cloud began to fight
More clouds arrived, both grey and black
And tried to stop the wind's attack

Then thunder roared, a frightful sound
And to the fight, he's quickly bound
And tangled with the winds great force
And tried to change its current course

The battle raged, the clouds on high
Twists and turned and raced on by
The little cloud, the first I spied
Opened her eyes and cried and cried

The other clouds, now dark with rage
Were trapped, as if within a cage
And they too, cried for all their worth
To soak the grounds of Mother Earth.

Corset is

The whale upon the ocean blue
A mammoth creature this is true
But a harpoon brings him down to size
And man has claimed for himself a prize

This blubber now, no more a whale
Just flesh and bone, exposed and pale
The blubber boiled, for oil to trade
The bones, of which, corsets are made

The female, now she's getting older
With the age, she's getting bolder
A tummy now, she must not show
Then into a corset she must go

The waist looks thin, a smile is showing
Dress and skirts are really flowing
But when the corset has been eased
The tummy heads towards her knees.

Covid-19

From Wuhan it came, like a thief in the night
The scourge from the East, gave the world such a fright
Corona virus brought with it, the shadow of death
Coughs and disease, and shortness of breath

A pandemic it was, as it ran through the land
Contagious on high, as it went hand to hand
Elderly and frail were the hardest it hit
Next on its list were those not so fit

Thousands a day, died throughout the land
Nurses and doctors were there giving a hand
Countries shut down, borders all closed
Shops and nursing homes cleansed and hosed

Millions worldwide contracted the disease
It spread through the world just at its ease
The army called in to assist in the fight
To keep people at home to lessen the spike

From what we can see, from the battle we fight
Is a long road ahead before we see light?
Scientists the world over, seek a vaccine
To release one and all from our forced quarantine.

Covid Bells

Covid bells, covid bells, Santa may not come
No more biscuits, no more rum
Covid makes the nose so red
With aches within the head

Covid changed his name, we're told
It's Delta that takes the hold
Delta doesn't need a sleigh
While we all need to pray

Running through the land
Like a red hot newfound band
Spreading germs and fear
To all who we hold so dear

Delta bells, Delta bells
Making our life hell
We will get you in the end
On this you can depend.

Cricket

Cricket is a popular game, amongst our men and women
A rival to our water game, the crawl or breast-stroke swimming
Cricket is a simple game, uses bat and ball and wicket
With official umpires watching out, having won their ticket

The bowler tries in many ways, to get the batsman out
A ball is bowled, at angry pace, and then let's out a shout
The batsman has missed the ball, it's hit him on the pad
The umpire gives a decision, you've been given out, my lad

There many other fielders, in this game yet to name
The men who field in slips, usually get the fame
Another one at square leg and third man way down there
One man on the boundary, he'd be rather square

As this game continues, and many maidens bowled
The runs are coming slowly, but boring, to be told
The wicket keepers waiting, a wicket is his aim
The bowler runs in quickly, but sadly ends up lame

This game, it isn't over, till everyone is bowled
Many are the stories, and many more is told
Of the batsman or the bowler, covered by their fame
In this game of cricket, it's a gentleman's game.

Crumpet

Let out shopping, yet again
Though my legs are racked with pain
Into Coles we went to buy
Lots of goodies and custard pie

As I walked in through the store
Christmas goodies by the score
No trollies, me, I've got some bags
Soon grabbed myself a tray of snags

With my roving eyes, I saw
Crumpets on special, twos and four
Grabbed two packs and hobbled off
Shopping then, I had to stop

To the teller, off we go
Many shoppers, we're moving slow
Finally it's our time to pay
Got our docket, Di says stay

Stay, I do, she's checking fast
To the end she comes at last
The teller made a bad mistake
To the desk, with me in wake

Enquiries clerk spots the error
Hand to face, in mock terror
Refunds done, she hands to me
The crumpet pair, she said they're free

Quick as a flash, as I can be
Asked her to have crumpet with me
Stony faced, she turned and said
Take him home, with this I fled.

Cyclone Harold

What's the noise across the ocean?
Cyclone Harold, in turmoil motion
The island of Vanuatu is his aim
Destruction is his claim to fame

Wind and water within the eye
Black clouds forming across the sky
The islanders, in panic mode
Head off along the only road

Wind causes havoc to homes and shops
Thunder peels while rain falls, non-stop
Waves up high across the land
All on deck to lend a hand

The storm heads off across the sea
With Fiji now, not the place to be
Harold roars, lets out more steam
Is this for real, or a nightmare dream?

The Pacific Islands, one and all
React to Mother Nature's call
Praise to the Lord that they can see
Cyclone Harold exit across the sea.

Day of the sun

The tired old sun heads off to the west
Wrapped up in a cloud, he's off for a rest
Last rays of the sun, paints clouds in the sky
Lights up the sky before they too, die

Night races in to claim space left by the sun
Shadows soon follow, as if on the run
Darting and ducking and moving around
Putting a cover all over the ground

Night has moved in, silent it lay
While little night creatures already at play
The stars in the night, brightly they shine
Mother Nature at work, all things are fine

Night marches on, a gentle breeze blowing
Lights in the city already are glowing
Babes in their beds, asleep and adored
While drivers abound, foot to the board

Night animals abound, they're off to their lair
A little light creating along in the air
Rays of the sun soon seen in the east
Another nice day, the world is at peace.

Day's End

Dawn awoke from a night of deep sleep
And bringing with it, white clouds like sheep
Yellow streaks touching the sky
Sending shadows wherever the fly

Early morning a sight to be seen
Nestled in pockets, bright and so clean
Down on the water, shadows appear
Neatly arranged, where the ships steer

Into the day clouds disappear
Great is the sun, as it reappears
High in the sky, heads out to the west
To be ready for setting, one of the best

Sun now descending, a tiring day
Home now for rest, this I do pray
On to the waters, with a sunset we're blessed
Wonders of nature, it's one of the best.

Decision Time

Dear Susan, the time has come again, I fear
Has poetry been introduced again this year
I sit, with pen in hand, so I can write
About two bull frogs locked in fight

Or perhaps an eagle in flight, so high
The story of the little white cloud fly by
A boat upon the sea's fine motion
Or a liner fight the stormy ocean

It's limitless what can be written
By someone there, who's just been sitting,
Awaiting for the words "to go"
Then sets off to go with the flow

The pen is steady, the mind still strong
I'll continue writing, be it right or wrong
Ninety-two years are in the past
Only the Lord knows how long I last.

Deep Reflections

I walked out on a well-worn track
Sun shone down upon my back
A breeze blows in across the lake
While ducks and swans are on the make

I spied upon a garden chair,
A lady sitting, with greying hair
A picture held in a work worn hand
On her finger lay a wedding band

As she watched that picture too
A tear appeared in eyes of blue
Deep reflections, I could tell
As clear to me, as if a bell

I stood back, my eyes felt dim
Sure that she was thinking of him
And how their lives had been just one
All she's left is a teen age son

She looked at me, gave a simple smile
I could see she's been around a while
Through it all, she's still tall and slim
It is plain she still walks with him

She looks up into a cloudless sky
As if to say a last "goodbye"
Turns and walks back along that track
I know then that she'll be back.

Delta

From Wuhan, China it had fled
A pandemic which has quickly spread
Across the world at rapid speed
It's what we see and what we read

Death and illness left in its wake
Vaccines then we had to take
To clear this threat and clean the air
To make the world and people care

Then Delta came, with flame and fire
Puts our risks up even higher
We struggle on, there's millions dead
Not knowing now what lays ahead

Wuhan had cleared the Alpha strain
But Delta raised its head again
Then like a boomerang, it charged
Right into Wuhan it has barged.

Devoted

It's been a struggle, but I've reached old age
I look back on life, it's like a drama on stage
Mother's life was hell, so she must be in heaven
Tending to Dad and the children of seven

No favourites for her, she gave of her best
Fed and schooled us, we were so blessed
Though at the time, we thought she was hard
Bless you my dear, words from a bard

My life, I know, was moulded by her
As were my siblings, treated so fair
Words of advice were willingly shared
The cane, when needed, not liberally spared

Through depression, and the war years
Caused concern and some fears
Through those years, she gave us hope
And as she said, "give enough rope"

Health was not great, but she battled on
Content with visits from daughter or son
Until that day that I said my goodbyes
She rests now with God in his skies.

Dinner Time

The kookaburra on tree top high
Waiting for old snake to pass by
Old snake has seen it all before
He knows that story of snake lore

He'll slither out when things are right
Keeping kookaburra well in his sight
He ventures out, beside a log
Waiting there for the green frog

The kookaburra, with laughter, sings
Makes a flap, with tired wings
Aware of where old snake is staying
And of the plans that he is making

The snake has got the frog in sight
Ready to take him in one bight
The frog hops off, the snake strikes out
He's got that frog firm, within his mouth

The Kookaburra, with eyes aglow
Takes in the action, far below
Dives on down, the snake he's caught
A snake for dinner is his thought.

D is for Doctor

D is for doctor, we see when we're sick
If we're not happy, we can give them the flick
There's plenty of doctors, just look in the book
You only need them when you're feeling crook

We don't have to pay, or just by the card
For we are in front, at least by a yard
If we're real sick and feeling so ill
I'm sure they will prescribe a soluble pill

If you get dire, a specialist they'll call
And Medicare, I'm sure, will take up the fall
If all this fails, there's an ambulance on hand
And in the hospital you'll ultimately land

As we get older, we're out every day
Visiting the doctor or some other health way
I admit it's not nice, feeling so ill
If the doctor don't get you the undertaker will.

Doctor, Oh Doctor

I went to my doctor the other day
To see what wisdom she had to say
As I walked in, she said I looked crook
I'll have to check up in my little black book

Put a band round my arm, pumped up the lead
I'd rather be chasing a runaway steed
With a frown on her brow, I wonder what's up
She said you've been drinking, but not from a cup

Next was a thing she put down through my vest
A check of my heart, she said it was next
My heart, she then said, that it is now read
I nearly freaked out, for I thought she said "dead"

Checked in my mouth, said, poke out your tongue
That got me in trouble, when I was so young
So I did as was told, it was covered in white
Said, put it back in, it's not a nice sight

I'm not doing well, this I could tell
Next thing I know she's ringing a bell
Nurse hurries on in, white as a sheet
Help me get this man up on to his feet

On to the bed, they helped me to get
My body was covered with heat and with sweat
With fingers so cold, she probed in my belly
Then made a quote "it's just like a jelly"

I'm off from the table and out through the door
Had enough of this jabbing, can't stand any more
Out of her office I travelled so far
To tell of my torture at my favourite bar.

Don't Drink and Drive

Don't drink and drive, it's often said
For who will know, if you turn up dead
Behind the wheel, or even broom
Always prevent the inevitable doom

If you drink, then walk a while
Don't end up on coroners file
Enjoy your drink, enjoy your ale
Then don't drive, you could end in jail

You could take a flagon home
Or are you afraid of wifie's moan?
The other option is, my mate,
Leave devil drink, change your fate.

Do You Remember?

Do you remember, when the earth seemed small
When trees and mountains were the only things tall
You'd buy a home for a thousand pounds
With shrubs and gardens within the grounds

We'd go to school in patched hand-me-downs
Which only caused occasional frowns
Our feet were bare, no shoes we had
But things in all were not too bad

No telephones in the houses yet
A public one, on the corner, sat
The radio was new to us
But no one seemed to make a fuss

When an aeroplane flew overhead
It carried passengers, we had read
Those who had a motor car
Were in the minority and by far

Potatoes, carrots, onions too
Into a bowl to make rabbit stew
The gardens on our household plot
Grew vegetables for our hungry lot

At the bottom of our garden, too
Stood the outhouse, just a lonely loo
Cleared each Monday, on the dot
Whether it was used or not

Then World War Two was thrust on us
With battle cries and all that stuff
Our lives were changed, I must agree
From poverty soon we were free.

With ships and cars and planes on high
Put more life beneath blue skies
But what a cost this war had brought
With men and women, who had fought!

With the peace once more restored
Men and women, in their hordes
Faced a fresh and better life
Enjoyed their time of man and wife.

Dreamer

He stands upon the rocky shore, casting eyes upon the seas
Pictures in his mind remembered, and visions that he sees
Recalls the early sailing ships, propelled by winds and gales
And of the whaling ships, as they hunted for the whales

Of the early prison ships, bound for Botany Bay
And of the many ships, lost along the way
Battle ships, in latter days, as they go off to war
To World War I and World War II, even to the Boar

Cruise liners now use the seas, as touring they do go
Taking passengers here and there, as only guides do know
The waves upon the ocean wave, beneath a sky of blue
With a little luck, I'm sure, I could be a dreamer too.

Dream on

Went down to the club the other day
Met a blonde lass on the way
She told me of her daily life
Not content to be someone's wife

We had a drink and had some fun
I told her jokes, an occasional pun
The night drifts on, it's time to go
Rain comes down, the wind does blow

Towards my car, I hurry fast
Only soon to be over passed
Into my car, she dives right in
Here's my time to fight off sin

No kiss or cuddle do I get
Haven't time to even fret
We headed home, to hers, of course
But after all, things could be worse

She opened the door, went right in
I felt that I'm out on a limb
I followed her to get a hug
She turned and said "Dream on, mug"

Dreams

If I had a ship, I'd sail away
To a foreign land with a sandy bay
As I have no ship, I'm prone to dream
That is how my life may seem

As a captain, I could sail at will
Each day to bring a newfound thrill
An ocean there for me to ride
As I watch the waves of a changing tide

The buccaneers in days of old
As they plundered for heaps of gold
Then hurried off, when things got hot
To avoid the blast of a naval shot

There's Captain Cook, who sailed down
Searching the seas for newfound ground
To claim it all for the distant crown
To receive acclaim on return to town

These thoughts pass through this head of mine
As I stand here, with the sun so fine
And dream the dreams of what could be
If I were a lad of twenty-three.

Drought Relief

Neath the shade of an old gum tree
Where the cattle wandered free
Across the land so harsh and brown
With little grass upon the ground

Summer sends its heated rays
Upon the trees and grass, it preys
Rain out here all but forgotten
Dams and lakes almost rock bottom

Hopes are for a bright tomorrow
Or to the banks, for cash to borrow
Stockmen with their eyes up high
Searching for clouds in the sky

Another week of desperation
On this, once lush, cattle station
For to the markets, stock must go
Just to ease the money flow

Clouds upon the southern slopes
Rain is what the stockman hopes
Thunder and lightning send a warning
Could be rain before the morning

With a week of drenching rain
All across the western plain
Hopes are high, there's more to come
To bring more work on this cattle run.

Dunny Out Back

I remember the time, with the dunny out back
I'd walk through the garden, down a short track
The smell and the flies, would show me the way
Always the same, be it at night or the day

It's one thing in life that I'll never forget
To sit on a hole, over a deep pit
The flies buzz around, as if in a dance
Waiting to land, if given the chance

We've progressed in life, of this I am sure
A toilet indoors, with a tight shutting door
Disinfectant and sprays, displayed for us all
Paper in rolls, neatly hang from the wall

These things maybe nice, but I still recall
The time of the dunny, with no rolls on the wall
And many's the time, through the garden I'd fall
Just taking myself to our dunny at nightfall.

Dusk to Dawn

Dusk to dawn, during the hours of dark
Werewolves and yeti let out their bark
Children lay sleeping, in their small bed
Ghosts play with those who are dead

Mysterious lights show, while we are asleep
Night noises rumble away in the deep
The devil is laughing, he's waiting for you
The man in the moon is looking on too

Night shadows creep, slowly at best
While I lay in bed, trying to rest
A groan is heard, as I nod off to sleep
Enough to make a grown man weep

A large light in the sky, the sun, I believe
I still am alive, there's much to relieve
I'll do it again, in twelve hours or more
It's the pattern of life, of this I am sure.

Early Days

It was on the banks of the Gloucester River
That my brother, he and I
Wet our fishing lines
To the tune of the silver eye

There were mullet, perch and catfish
Turtles and the eels
But a stack of flamin' water
As we battled with our reels

It was in these very waters
That our rabbit gut, we'd throw
Then the slashing of the waters
Showed the eels were on the go

Then with garden forks we'd spike them
To the bank we'd quickly toss
We would skin and gut 'em
Then we'd hand 'em to the boss

She would fry the meat, we'd eat it
With some bread, dipped in oil
Then contented we could start
As we prepared ourselves for toil.

Early Life

Life was hard in the depression years
Many a life had been turned to tears
No work to be had, in the country towns
Most food grown in the back yard grounds

Men took rod and reel to the local stream
If no fish caught they could at least dream
Rabbit traps set for their fur and meat
While mother, at home, kept the home neat

Swagmen with their rolls on back
Called at homes for a hand-out pack
For payment they would chop some wood
Or any tasks that they could

Life carried on this way for years
Until Hitler filled our hearts with fears
Lives changed then for all that day
Work for all and make Hitler pay

Four long years we had to wait
Before we heard of Hitler's fate
Then Japan we had to fight
Fighting them with all our might

Troops returned to their home towns
Music, laughter, joyous sounds
Life now filled with working men
Let's hope this peace will never end.

Eighty Years On

It's eighty long years, I remember it well
Like a chapter you read in a letter from hell
The sixth of June, in the year forty-four
The battle that won the war, it is sure

From the shores of Britain, in boats they came
The skies were so clear, no sign of rain
English, Canadians, the Americans force
Heading for France and Normandy course

The Nazis were waiting, hidden from view
Our boats were still coming, they had no clue
As they approached, guns roared from the shore
The enemy, in cover, let out a roar

Bodies were falling, blood everywhere
Sun covered by smoke, thick in the air
Over bodies and boulders, the attack carried on
No thought of retreat, this must be won

Days and nights, the battle draws on
No thoughts for men, be it brother or son
A victory, it must be, for the world at large
Just keep moving, like a slow-moving barge

D Day had arrived, this battle is won
But what of the cost of father or son
With eighty years on, we remember it well
And many a story of bravery still tell.

E is for Earth

E is for Earth, with its gold sandy beaches
Snow covered mountains, where man seldom reaches
Rivers that run right down to the oceans
Seas that move with the gentlest of motions

Lands that produce the grains and the grasses
Birds and frogs that live in the marshes
Cascading rivers to make waterfalls
Among the green bushes a bellbird calls

Summer appears with the heat and the sun
Autumn follows with time for a run
Winter to bring the snows and the chills
Soon Spring is upon us with laughter and thrills

Moonlight turns things into silvery grey
Shadows dancing along as they play
Night arrives with birds in their nests
Safely away from four legged pests

Morning has broken, sun shining bright
Gone is the darkness, held over night
An ocean of blue, stately at rest
This is the time that I love the best.

Emergency Room

Upon this hospital bed I lay
While nurse and doctor have their say
Then into my hand a needle goes
While soon my red blood starts to flow

E C G was my next test
I tried so hard to be my best
But soon I heard the machine beep
As I stood up upon my feet

Blood pressure was the next to go
Twice they did it, in a row
For once, her hand was on my knee
My pressure was not what it should be

The doctor then, came to fix my pain
To him, he said, it is quite plain
The trouble with your tummy, mate
You have played and lost with fate.

Endings

My story is ending, but my life is not done
I've still got time for fun in the sun
In the time that I have left, I'll live it the best
I'll live each day, between work and rest

My mind is still active, but my action is slow
I'll do what I can and let the rest go
Take one day at a time, I've heard it said
I'll be alright, as long as I'm fed

The road that I've followed, throughout my life
Has broadened the mind and settled the strife
With the good and the bad, I've had my share
But after it all, many good times were there

Now I sit back to see what's in store
My bones are aching, my flesh is so sore
I'll wait for the calling, with this I am fine
Until that day, when the Lord has called "time".

English

I must ask about this English, and how it came about.
If you weren't bought up with, it would really
    make you shout.
When I talk about a ewe, I'm not talking about you,
I'm talking about an animal that has four legs, not
    two.

When speaking of the word called to, is it too or two?
Many times we see it spelt to, when it should have
    been too.
A golfer, when he makes a strike, is known to call
    out "fore"
Four people standing together are asked, "What are
you waiting for?"

The numbers keep on flowing; I've come to number
    eight.
Then I ask the question, perhaps it's something that
    you ate?
I also have a problem with the word wind, or is it
    wind?
When I took my lady out, after dinner we were
    wined.

I went to the butcher's, there a lady I did meet.
Then when I got home, I was asked "where's the
    meat?"
With the Aussie English, we're really tempting fate,
We open up a convo, with "'ow ya goin', mate?"

E. R. Again

They sent me off to E. R. again
They seem to think I am the pain
The questions they ask, I already know
But I go along, just let it flow

Last name, first name, what bought you here
Birth date, address, what's there to fear
Where is the pain, what is it like?
Does it hurt more riding a bike?

Blood pressure taken, it's really quite low
Keep your arm still, let the blood flow
E C G hooked up, with cords everywhere
The readings are taken, just hang on in there

An hour has passed, you're left there to rest
Rest did she say? There's too many pests
So lay there I must, and wait for the Doc
And while I wait, I'm watching the clock

The Doc comes along, more questions for me
He seems to think my heads all at sea
They're doing their best, what more can I ask
It seems my problems are the same as the past.

Faces

We're all getting old, or so I've been told
I look in the mirror and what do I behold
A face looking back, that I once knew
Not looking now, as when it was new

The ravage of time and the ageing effect
Has woven the pattern, but there's no regrets
For over the years, many places I've been
Beautiful scenery and places I've seen

Some roads have been rough, others serene
I look at the bad and the good, as I dream
I'm now on the downhill, my foot on the brake
I remember the time when I was a young rake

Life's getting weary, I now sit in the sun
Remember the time when life was such fun
I've not given up, still life for the living
Still have the urge for loving and giving

That face in the mirror, I seem to recall
Has been with me, since I was quite small
I know every line and mark on that face
Even the causes and where they took place

If I were to be given a rerun of life
I'd probably repeat my errors and strife
Then look at the face in the mirror once more
And think of my life, as I have done before.

Fangs for the Fish

The lad, he went a fishing, a fishing he did go
With rod and reel and fishing line, all there on show
Put the bait upon the hook, gave a mighty toss
Then sat back and waited, he'd show the fish who's boss.

The river wide and muddy, no thought upon his mind
Just sat back and waited, wondered what he'd find
The cork, it went a-bobbing, the line became quite taut
Our lad behind the fishing, wondered what he'd caught.

Upon his feet he stumbled, slack line winding in;
Within in the muddy waters, he thought he saw a fin
The fight was on in earnest, the battle lines were drawn
The biggest fish he'd sighted, since the day that he was born.

Their struggle carried onwards, the night was drawing in
The fish had reached the surface, splashed and made a din
But the fisherman of the moment, reeled the monster out
He lay back then, exhausted, and let out a final shout.

The journo's grabbed his story, cameras flashing bright
Telling of his story, and of his massive fight
Today he lives in splendour with photos on his wall
Neighbours tell the story of the fish upon his wall.

Farewell Red Rocket

It's with sadness that I tell you
That my heart is nearly breaking
For my mind is in a Twitter
With the decision that I am making

It's with tears upon the eye lids
I say "farewell, red rocket"
As I change it for another
I'll keep its spare key in my pocket

Although I know it's gone forever
But in my heart, it will remain
Now I'll have to train my new Suzuki
Then I'll sing its sweet refrain

It's gone where good cars go
No longer on lease
But buried so deep
Poor old thing, may it RUST in peace.

Farmer Brown

The local wag is farmer Brown
Known far and wide all over town
Owns a farm on the riverbanks
Has no time for the local cranks.

On that farm he had some hens
Donated eggs to his best friends
One hen in particular would not lay
He said, "my God, I'll make you pay"

Next Sunday then, he made her lay
Upon a plate of white and grey
Around the table, each had to pray
Then ate the hen that would not lay.

The moral of this story then
Is if you choose to be a hen
Lay your eggs within your nest
Then at night it's perfect rest.

Fires

It was red in the morning and red in the night
As we watched the firemen fighting their fight
Smoke in the sky, no sun to be seen
Ash just remains where houses had been

Towns have burned down, no water to spare
Grasses all burnt, trees standing there bare
The birds of the forest are not to heard
Of the poor old koala not even a word

One thousand homes lost in one week
Tired firefighters asleep on their feet
No relief is in sight, more still to come
Record temperatures sent from the sun

Many lives lost, and fires still burn
Who will be next? Where will we turn?
Food and supplies in desperate need
And for the cattle, where is their feed

Another day, with more fires spread,
Bush so burnt and looking so dead
Leaves and debris carried on high
To start new fires, wherever they lie

Dear Lord in Heaven, please hear our plea
Send down some rain, on land and on sea
To replenish this land and make it so green
Restore it again, to what it had been.

Footprints

Upon the lounge room wall I see
Footsteps that's been made by me
For I've been tearing out my hair
And cranky as a grizzly bear

For isolation, I'm sad to say
Is not the way for me to play
I wish to be upon the sea
Riding waves, and drinking tea

But coronavirus has got me tied
Within my home I must abide
Until a vaccine can be found
I'm afraid that I'm homeward bound

The world is such a sorry place
Cannot even show our face
To see the world, it's tele-view
I'm ready now to throw a shoe.

When I go to bed at nights
I dream of all the ugly sights
They show upon the Tele screen
Makes me want to let out a scream.

Footy Finals

There're ten footy teams fighting for glory
This is the start and the end of the story
Storm from the south, with brimstone and fire
Challenge the rest with form and desire

The Eels splash around, slipping and sliding
Are they one of those getting a hiding?
The team from the East, with silver tail backing
Will they get there or will they show lacking

The black and the green, the South Sydney side
Will they be trying, or just for the ride?
There's Sharks galore, but they've been before
Hard to think they will return for some more

The Panthers are breathing away in the west
Will they be ready to meet with the best?
Red and blue of the Newcastle Knights
Will one of the teams put out their lights?

Manly, the team that everyone hates
Spurred by fans and a few of their mates
Titans, of course, from up in the north
They could surprise and come to the fourth

The Raiders, the fearsome green machine
This the best that Canberra have seen
Ten strong and vital football teams
On paper, that is the way it seems

Regardless of the outcome, money is King
May the one strongest, achieves a great win
After fight and folly, it's really a shame
For football, as we know it, is only a game.

Framed

I saw today a picture frame
Six ladies then, along they came
To make a picture, oh so fine
Now we see, it's etched in time

The ladies in their finery
Covered there from neck to knee
Put a smile upon their face
Filled the frame with love and grace

If you should wish to happen by
Then catch the frame within your eye
There's a picture there for you to make
A photo then for one to take.

Fred

A man of his calibre is hard to find
One who had such an inquisitive mind
Could tunnel his thoughts into big or small
To the rest of us, he's ten feet tall

A request for help was often heard
He's the first with a helping word
With eyes afire and smile so bright
Would work on a problem half the night

Computer pals, was his great love
Helping people, he'd give a shove
Prose and verse, his real acclaim
Never a thought of praise or fame

A humble man, through his long life
Helped along by a loving wife
But the Lord in heaven called his name
It's time for Fred to leave earth's game.

Freedom

At last, they say "We are free to go out"
The house re-echoes with "free" I do shout
But steady is the way we're told to behave
So clean up, I must, and have a close shave

So clean clothes I don, and out into the sun
My first steps shaky, but I'm ready for fun
I'm off to the shops, hope there's plenty to see
But things, I find, are not like they use to be

Stop marks on the floor, at which I must stay
Then with a plastic they want me to pay
From a distance, they ask "what do I need"
The answer, my friend, a tasty new feed

A bottle of sanitiser, they point out to me
Squeezed on my hands, seems what it's to be
A roll of towelling on a rack, next I'm shown
This seems to be the norm all over town

Half hour of shopping, I'm really worn out
I want to go home, I'm ready to pout
This type of shopping is really a pain
I just going home and be locked up again.

Freedom Day

We're free, we're free, I hear you say
We're free to do all things today
Join our friends, do as we like
Go to the beach or ride a bike

Lockdown now a thing of the past
Life goes on, we're learning fast
Kids back at school, what a relief
Almost seems like it's beyond belief

But spare a moment, if you've the time
To cast your mind on a different line
The sick, the old in a nursing home
All of those, no more to roam

They're condemned to lockdown daily
No freedom here for man or lady
If you think that freedoms fair
Within your freedom, could you share?

Free Verse

There was this dream
I know not what
Was I going up
Or coming down?

We do not know, it's not the time
Tomorrow is another day
I wonder who is gonna pay.

I asked my dad
What should do?
Do, he said, do what is right
Who is the judge, I wonder now

It's time for bed, I must go
To the land of Nod
Goodnight my friend.

Frogs

A frog went out for his daily walk
Sidled up, said he wants to talk
He wears a coat of green and brown
Claims he's known all over town

I kept my distance, stepped back a pace
He advanced, right in my face
Told me a tale of his little pool
He must thing I'm a silly fool

He babbled on, told me what he sought
Then told me of other frogs he's fought
Promised a home, with a water view
Under a sky of azure blue

He told me more of his little spot
Where winters cool and summer hot
Then told me that I looked so nice
Wants to make me his own wife

I answered yes, what could I say?
Then hurried off to his secluded bay
Today I have tadpoles by the score
Boys or girls, well I'm not sure.

From My Balcony

In the early part of day
Drifting in across the bay
A heavy drift of morning mist
With a gentle whirling twist

Around the mountain side, it sits
Like a mini skirt exists
Sunshine upon it, shining bright
Birds scattered as in fright

Many figures can be seen
In this, a fine mountain scene
A gentle breeze passes by
Lifting mist up into the sky

Soon the mist has risen high
Up into a cloudy sky
Where it mingles with the clouds
Seems now that it's wrapped in shrouds

Dark clouds over mountain tops
Light rain falls in certain spots
Then as if by magic flow
Sun shines through, soon clouds go.

George and Dragon

He stood outside the St George and dragon
Just arrived in his horse drawn wagon
Lips are drawn from his want of beer
Saw the dragon and cringed in fear

You'll not get a drink in here, she said
Not if you're alive, or even dead
So be off with you, you worthless cur
Or I'll pull your whiskers, hair by hair

The poor man then, with courage fading
I want to see George, and not the dragon
Lowered his head and barged right in
Looking for safety with George, within

The dragon followed, not to be outdone
Watched by others, who saw the fun
She grabbed him by his collar, white
Started off with a ding dong fight

George to the rescue, with his gun
Broke up the watcher's morning fun
A blast of the gun to clear the air
But frightened off his customer's mare

Out the door, the customer ran
Chasing after his wayward van
That was the last they saw of him
He'd found himself a friendly Inn.

Get Online

Scones and cream and coffee galore
Bought crowds in within the door
To learn the lessons by tutors there
Taking selfies with utmost care

Many came in to learn the tricks
While a few just came along for kicks
The mobile phones were out in numbers
While some, I'm sure, were deep in slumber

Get online, the message said
Other info, then I had read
It's all to help our seniors out
And see what marvels are about

Tea and scones had soon departed
Then the photo show had started
The President, with the mouse in hand
Showed the snaps, oh so grand

Time was short and soon run out
With people moving all about
One and all enjoyed the day
Where everybody had their say.

God's Waiting Room

We live in a village, on a road we all share
There's fifteen units, some singles, some pairs
The ambos all know us; they're often in here
We're close to a club, for those who need beer

There're six pair of kneecaps recently repaired
There're wheelchair and walker for the impaired
Glasses on noses, two dozen at least
But we all get together for our Christmas feast

Pacemakers are needed for some of our flock
We all take our pills, all by the clock
A chemist we have, just round the bend
A doctor close be, to us he does tend

There're crutches and canes and other health aids
With VA and Medicare are the ones that put paid
For we are in limbo, and knowing that soon
We're all just sitting, in Gods waiting room.

GN (Goodnight)

For sixty years Morse has been dead
No sign of it to raise its head
No more the dots and dashes heard
Not now with Morse, a single word

The men who worked the morse code key
Remember how it used to be
Then listen to the sounder work
Taking messages was just a lurk

Then as the years have come to pass
With men who worked there in the past
Their ages now is eighty plus
They move around with little fuss

They know that when it's time to go
They'll hear the message, oh so low
For they will not put up a fight
And sign off with their last GN.

Gran

She sits upon her old rocking chair
A bun tied up in her long white hair
On a wrinkled face, a far-away look
In her hands, lay a photo book

Next to her, sits a vacant chair
It's been empty for nearly a year
She'll glance across then glance away
No one there, with her to stay

The mind returns some sixty years
When they exchanged love, and maybe tears
Joined as one, for the years ahead
Until that day when he lay dead

Her thoughts return to her family tree
Eleven boys and girls ran free
Her eldest son, she gave to me
A greater dad is yet to be

A tear upon an eyelid shows
The strength within the eyes still glows
For the one who's gone to pastures green
And thoughts of life, and what it had been

I look back and see her there
A still strong woman, there with care
I thank the Lord for giving me
A grandma, proud for all to see.

Gran's Old Rocker

It stands in the corner, so dark and forlorn
Seems to have stood there since Adam was born
The screws have worked loose, paint now is so thin
This is the rocker that Granny sat in

When she was around, she'd sure make it go
While knitting or sewing, she'd rock to and fro
Her hair, she had, tied up in a bun
If the cat saw her there, he'd take off and run

She'd rule the house, from in that same chair
And dish out her orders to anyone there
Grandfather's life, she made it a hell
He'd have to come running, when she rang her bell

She had a sixth sense, she knew what you think
And many's the time your feelings would sink
But under it all is a soft-hearted wench
Loved making cakes on her work worn bench

Now Granny's passed on, I'll repair her old chair
Getting it ready for when I lose my hair
I'll have it all ready for when I get old
Then I can do my own rock and roll.

Gravity Pull

Once upon a time, when I was young
Everything in place and nothing hung,
Muscles taut and I'm gung-ho
Nothing then I had on show.

My girlfriend too, she was a beaut
A 38 breast that looked so cute.
Her body showed her clothes so neat
Being classy was a simple feat.

We had fun, our bodies so trim
Changed our clothes on a whim
A bikini was the thing to wear
The thing to make others stare,

The years roll on, life takes its toll
Different to when I was on a roll,
My girlfriend now is 38 down
All she gets is a worried frown.

This story is for one and all.
Go out, enjoy and have a ball.
Tomorrow then when gravity draws
Worry not, for it's still all yours.

Green and Gold

They wear, with pride, their green and gold
A story true and should be told
Of those that left our Aussie shores
With many hopes and much applause

The Olympic Games in Paris, bound
And all the joys there, to be found
There's swimmers, runners and many more
To bring back medals to our fair shore

The swimmers bring our greatest hope
With other countries, they must cope
But give the girls and boys their fare
They'll come through with time and care

The starter's gun and off they go
With all their training now on show
Back and forth, the meters pass
Green and gold have shown their class

The medal count goes on and on
Gold and silver and of bronze
For our athletes, you can be sure
There's yet to be so many more

When it's over, games are done
Time is now for lots of fun
We thank Paris for being there
To show Advance Australia Fair.

Gus is Missing

In the north of South Australia, where very little grows
A thousand miles of nowhere, just the wind that blows
This semi desert flatland with sand and stunted shrubs
A little boy gone missing, a lad the family loves

Gus, the lad in question, an explorer of the land
Out to check the country, seeing things first-hand
In his seek for knowledge and investigative mood
Went his way undaunted, without water or of food

The parents at the homestead, realising things were wrong
Searched around the station, were searching all day long
Alarm spreads through the area, searchers by the score
Checking through the section, even through the local bore

The day turns into nightfall, nothing had been seen
In the days that follow, with horses and machines
Vast areas had been covered, without sight or sound
Little Gus has vanished, no more he's homeward bound

A footprint in the desert, a tracker on the trail
Another night of worry, another day of fail
The search continues onward, numbers decreased
Recovery now the order, from a police release.

Haiku One

(Japanese poetry of 3 lines, 17 syllables, describing something in nature)

Baby into bath
Suds around for baby's fun
Dried and nappies then

Pussy chasing cat
Received then, a playful smack
Knows that cats fight back

Kitten chasing mouse
In and out they battle on
All around the house

Little kitten lost
Pussy, pussy oh so sweet
Come and live with me

Horse so big and strong
Working in the heat of day
Nose bag full of chaff

Day's end draws closer
Waiting the sight of sunset
Night draws the curtains

Sunrise morning shines
Over hills and valleys bright
Day and night follows.

Haiku Two

(Japanese poetry of 3 lines, 17 syllables, describing something in nature)

Zebra on the plain
Watching the zebra crossing
Traffic thick as rain

Lions on the prowl
Their meals on four legs again
No meal arrived, tough

Crocodile in creek
What's on for midday dinner?
Under water, croc waits

A giraffe on high
With his eyes upon the sky
Watching clouds go by

Rod held, nervous hands
Fish upon the waters, swim
Catch upon riverbank

Gentle waters, flow
Swimmer into waters, jump
Water shallow, bang

An amazing place
Where surf, sea and sun abounds
Mother Nature paints.

Haiku Three

(Japanese poetry of 3 lines, 17 syllables, describing something in nature)

Gentle, the rain fell
Wetting the grass and the trees
Sun then stopped the rain

The sun shines brightly
Beauty we see every day
Night comes sun at rest

Sunrise over lake
Boats at rest on calm water
Sunset cast shadows

Shadows in the day
Casting pictures in the black
Shadows gone with night

Clouds upon blue sky
Gently flowing on the blue
Wind comes, all clouds go

Wind in the willow
Leaves floating on rivers flow
Autumn comes, tree bare

Beauty surrounds us
Lovely to the beholder
A sight to be viewed

The world around us
Wrapped in beautiful surrounds
A joy to be seen.

Happy Easter

May Easter bring you all you wish
Whether it's chocolates or be it fish
The Easter Bunny with all his guile
Will be around, in his usual style

With chocolates, lollies or Easter Eggs
But little thought to him, he begs
To be among his Easter friends
And with you, his wish to blend

This Easter then, with lots of joy
Whether it be girl or boy
The parents too come into this
And enjoy our Easter wish.

He's Heading Home

He's heading off, down the dusty road
On his back, once was a heavy load
The hair, what's left, is snowy white
Still, on his cheek is the golden light

As his mind flashes back to his early years
A tear appears in the eyes, still clear
When as a boy, his life flowed so sweet
And what, in life, will he have to meet

To school he went to gain his knowledge
No monies spare for a course at college
School days ended and work begun
Days at work, just weekend fun

A wife and two was next to come
More work needed, he's on the run
Bought a home, to the bank he turned
Took all the money he had earned

Forty years he worked and toiled
Cleared all bills, bankers foiled
Retirement came, a void to fill
Some then say, you're over the hill

Travel then, was next in line
Sailing seemed to fit in fine
Ships and planes came to the fore
Till age caught up, travel no more

He's heading now, down the road to home
Not much more left for him to roam
With heavy heart he awaits his friend
Come home son, you've reached the end.

High Noon

We've heard rumblings from Canberra
And have heard the knives are out.
For the Liberals of this country
Know what the noise is all about.

We have heard it on radio, also on T.V.
The clash of personalities that show
And the struggle for the leader
For this country that we know

Our Prime Minster has been dethroned
By his members, front and back
Who have set out to destroy him.
Like the dingos in a pack

It was forty-five to forty
That has caused the present spill
And the loyalty and trust, well
He is looking for them still

He has reluctantly now decided
That at noon would be the time
That the forces faced each other
To see then who would sign

We find that Turnbull's been rejected
And there's a battle going on
With three of his old colleagues
Fight to see who'll be the one

Then when the battle is over
And the dust has settled down
Will there be any changes
By he, who wears the crown.

His New Boots

A husband, to the store, he went
A handful of money, he had spent
New pair of boots upon his feet
Thought the world was, oh so sweet.

Home he trots, new boots on show
Heart and head quite a glow.
"Wife my dear, look what I've got"
Turned to him, said, "not a lot"

Into bathroom he did go
A naked body is now on show.
The boots, of course, still exposed
But not a single piece of clothes.

To his wife, he went again
Brand new boots shown so plain
Upon her face is a worried frown.
"Your manly piece is hanging down"

The husband, now in danger mood
Almost burst out with something rude.
"It's my new boots, it's looking at"
Wife's reply, "you should have got a hat".

His Whiskers

He was tall and he was battered
He had tattooed legs and arms
Dressed in shorts and singlet
And sat, asleep and calm.

He had a beard like Santa's
But unkempt and let go wild.
He had hair upon his body
It looked dirty and so vile.

The barber viewed this person
Not knowing where to start,
But thought a country shearer
May play a better part.

But the barber, wise and tactful,
And showing not a care
Set in, attacked the whiskers
Which left his face so bare.

The barber shook him gently
He woke up with a roar,
Then cursed the frightened barber
For the reflection that he saw.

It's my hair that I need cutting
Not the whiskers on my face.
If you don't do something shortly
You will leave the human race.

The barber, red and sweating
Knee deep in human hair,
Stuttered out "I'm sorry"
As he gasped in more fresh air.

The man jumped up and shuddered
And headed for the door,
Then turned towards the barber
Said "I ain't returning here no more".

The barber, stunned and shell-shocked
Relaxed and had some beers
The thought of "ain't returning"
Was music to his ears.

Home Sweet Home

Weeks now, we have been locked in at home
Has given me time, with soap and with foam
To clear up the mess in my private den
For when we get out, is it if or is it when

I've trimmed the garden, it's looking quite nice
All done with advice, from my darling wife
Needless to say, she's more jobs for me
But rest while at home, isn't to be

Tiles are shining, the carpet so clean
Can't even see where my boot marks had been
Soon I'll have dinner to prepare and to make
Must remember my pills, these I must take

Works getting heavy, lots still to do
Cleaned out the fireplace, even the flu
Things are so shiny, not a thing out of place
Even the mirror, I can see my own face

Day after day I have a big dream
To have a sponge cake, with lots of cream
Yet for me, I'm locked up and so sad
I want to get out, it's driving me mad.

Houdini or Houdoggi

Caged away for protection and care,
Poor little puppy, his cage is so bare,
Watched a film of Houdini's escape
Up the wall and over the gate.

Not waiting around, to see how things fall
He's off into the garden, to play with a ball.
No lock up for him, he wants to be free
If someone comes after him, he'll surely flee.

When time comes around for him to be fed,
He'll grab something, then hide under the bed.
For love and attention, he'll go when he's ready,
The thing he misses most is his cuddly teddy.

If they lock him back in, he'll get out for sure
He'll not be locked in behind a wire door
Just treat me with love, don't lock me away
When I'm contented, I'll be home to stay.

How's That?

A match being played between India and Australia
Let us not talk of winning or of failure
The players WADE out to commence their innings
What's on their minds, it's got to be winnings

They're trying for BURNS to light up their play
Unfortunately for us he just couldn't stay
The SMITH of the side came in for some nicks
But only for nought, for he was caught in the slips

The HEAD of the pack, next man to come in
But he copped a ball fair on his shin
GREEN by name and green in his hitting
Top score to him, I think it quite fitting

PAYNE being felt by one and by all
Not having much luck with hitting the ball
The CUMMINS and goings are really so fast
Who's going to help them, how will they last?

A roar from the LYON, it'll be a walk in the park
For he'll get a hand from a fellow named STARC
But bat as they must, it just couldn't last
The Indians have scalped them, let's have a repast.

Hungry

If your starving, hungry and feel like a bite
Would you throat muscles clamp up so tight
Were you're a vegan, is there a toll
If you get your teeth into a Chicko roll

A cow in the paddock eats grass galore
Clover, or Lucerne or anything more
She is a vegan as well as you
So get stuck in and have a good chew

The grass in the meadow, so green and so lush
Let the stock in and they go with a rush
Eating the greenery that you so love
Enjoying the things that you want to have

One vegan to another, go for it mate
Don't worry about what is your fate
Eat up the meat before it's too late
I'll meet you in heaven at the pearly gate.

I Do Not Cough

You could hear her coming a mile away
Before you could even see her sway
Down the road you would hear her go
On the heal and then the toe

As she moved you'd hear her bark
Frightened the dogs around the park
Baying here and baying there
Taking in the clean, cold air

She'd cough and cough till her sides were sore
Making noise like a midnight snore
Coughs and spluttering as she'd go
To the doctors she should show

I've told her many times before
Be careful with the coughs you bear
For it's not the coughing that carries you off
But the coffin that they carry you off'in.

I Don't Think

At this time in life I find I don't have to think
I'm told what to do, in the flash of a wink
No, don't do that, do what I said
Or you'll end up with a clout on the head

I'm told to get up, first order today
Then if your good, with your iPad you play
My iPad, I find, does things of its own
Changes my words, to this it is prone

Between my iPad and boss
I tell you my friend, I'm not at a loss
They're both just along to ruin my life
Don't even help to lower my strife

Time to do dinner, this I am told
Just do the job and don't so bold
When I move over, it's Heaven, I'm planned
My time in hell, I've had on this land.

I Eye

The eyes of the world are looking at me
Is it because I'm not able to see
I try as I might, but sadly it seems
My life is locked up with wonderful dreams
My eyesight is good, it's just I don't see
I live in my world, a world that is free
I'm living each day, as if it's my last
Been living this way, from back in the past
The people around me, trying to guide
They say they are helpful and on my side
I wonder at times if it is worthwhile
But having said that, I'll give it a trial
A trial has been set, I'm willing to see
I think they may be able to help me.

If I Were a Fly

If I were a fly on the wall in the house
I'd get around as quiet as a mouse
Can you imagine the scene in the room
If it got out? I'm sure it would spell doom

I would fly, with the greatest of ease
Just anywhere, just like a breeze
Not a soul in the room would know I was there
I'd see it all, be it clothed or be it bare

The tales I could tell, would fill up a book
All readers then would take a quick look
I'm telling you, for the stories are right
But I must say that I've not learnt to write

The shame of it all, I could head for a fall
I must keep watching, though I'm tiny not tall
It's the one with aerosol can that I fear most
One spray of that stuff then I'm no longer a host.

I'm in Focus

I went to In Focus, to see what's inside
Down on my luck, but still have my pride
The tummy upset with wind and with pain
Don't want these needles again and again

Filled in some forms, don't know what for
Then I was grabbed and rushed through a door
Into a change room, removed lots of cloth
Wrapped in a gown, then met the boss

I'm Jemma, she told me, I'm here to help you
Onto a table and with a hole to go through
A jab in the arm, to help on the way
For all this trouble, I don't have to pay

So gentle, so easy, she handled me
Then into that hole, was all I could see
While a draft from the back, into my kilt
The shock was too much, I started to wilt

With Jemma in charge, what can I say
Onto my back, and there I must lay
Breathe in and hold it, was the command
Did as directed but heart in my hand

A beautiful smile on Jemma's red lips
Standing there, with hands on her hips
Your time is up, you've had your order
Go on home and have two cups of water.

In a bowl

I know what a fish feels like in a bowl
As I live here in my little hole
Around and around swimming he goes
While I sit around writing my prose

He's no need to hurry, he's going nowhere
While all of my doings are up in the air
He looks out at the sky, no clouds to be seen
I'd like to be out, of that I am keen

But like the poor fishy, I'm anchored at home
Like chains on my legs, I'm not able to roam
But my fish doesn't have the use of T.V.
I have the advantage, but there's little to see

When the virus is over and I am set free
I'd love to take my fish outside with me
But he wouldn't like it when I have my meal
Yet I'll always remember just how he must feel

Indian / Pacific (Reality)

On central station, we gather with glee
Some hundred people, and then there was me
Waiting to board this wonderful train
To cross the mountains and onto the plain

The platform was cold, but music galore
We're almost ready, just waiting for four
We're eager and ready, but still we wait
What lies ahead, what is our fate?

The train is now ready, we're ready to go
We wait with the others, then go with the flow
Off through the suburbs and into the hills
We hope for the best and hope there's no ills

Into the mountains, then to Lithgow we dash
Like Marjorie Jackson, Lithgow's own flash
Then Bathurst we head, but hit our first snag
A train broken down, announced a real wag

Sixty odd minutes we twiddled our toes
But could be worse if it's raining or snows
Again we are off, heading for Parkes
Once more the gremlins are playing their larks

Out in the salt bush, nothing in sight
Until there's an eagle, wings in full flight
Then into our window, head-first he burst
Our driver and off-sider let out a curse

An hour we waited until they replace
More waiting around, this we must face
Our timetable shot, with time to make up
We've worn out our quota of "our Lady Luck"

We call in at Cook, to have a good look
Weather cold and windy and really so crook
Back on the train and took off so fast
Left it behind and into the past

We though by this time our problems were over
And we would be in a bed of green clover
But wrong again, you hear me say
Let us all then, kneel down and pray

By midnight then, we've stopped yet again
We're all wracked with sleepless and pain
Three hours we wait and nothing is said
While I sweat in my doona topped bed

Head off again, hope no more fright
For we have Perth well in our sight
We left the train dressed and well fed
And, Oh, for tonight a stationary bed.

I Need a Hand

I need another hand, he said, my current two are full
The weight between my two, I can really feel the pull
There're roads around the world today, bridges everywhere
The one I like the best, is the one within my pair.

Tourists come from near and far, to see this magic sight,
Others come to see it, but tremble then in fright.
The sight within these hands, a vision there to see.
A sight across the mountains and to the distant sea.

The magic of the moment will live with you for life
While on this skyward roadway, you could take a wife.
This roadway up to heaven, in Vietnam's green lands,
You feel a part of heaven, is held within your hands.

In Isolation

In isolation and in beauty, stands a tree of tender years
Overlooking sea and water, as it wipes away the fears
Though its food supply is limited, it struggles, as we see
As for all the things in nature, it's to battle on and be

Rocks and stone, be it your fortress, in your isolated spot
Sea and sky add to your beauty, be the weather cold or hot
You remain in your defiance, as you battle sea and storm
But the beauty of your setting, adds to your natural form

You have picked a rocky coastline, to be calling it a home
And in times of cyclones, you can see the water's foam
Yet the tree, encased in rock form, battles on to be
One of the Creator's beauty spots, here by the tranquil sea.

In the Land of Snow

The miles fly by with regular ease
I miss the sight of Aussie gum trees
Fogs and mists and clouds in the sky
Reduce the vision of things that I spy

There's snow upon the mountain tops
And waterfalls that never stops
Then run across the permafrost
And through the trees till finally lost

The clouds on high create a scene
Like the sights upon a screen
Of elf's and goblins, in black and white
As they prance and dance and even fight

The rain that falls upon the ground
Is to the lakes and rivers, bound
It makes the land a verdant green
With sun and warmth, gives off a sheen

Towns and villages by the score
Some are beautiful, others a bore
If we don't go, how do we know?
So put on your glad rags, let's have a go.

Invisible Tribe

We are all part of the invisible tribe
It matters not, how hard we must strive
Be it the doctor, chemist or grocery store
Invisible are we, as walk through the door

Make an appointment, you sit and you wait
What is the verdict? What is my fate?
No one will worry what it's to be.
Doc doesn't care, he's getting his fee

Go to the chemist, there is a queue
Just have a chair, we've only a few
Others come in, they pass through so quick
My eyes deceived me, or is it a trick?

Off to the grocers, we hurry on past
Doing our shopping, we're quick and fast
Then join a line, we wait and we wait
I make a noise before they take the bate

How do you feel, you go through your chores
No one to help, as you pass through the doors
Retirees all, I tell you, my friends
Invisible we feel, until our lives end.

Is it Over?

Light can be seen at the tunnel's end.
Isolation is over, friend meet friend.
Steady she goes, step by step
Distance apart are still strictly kept.

Some businesses are open, others are not,
Masks not compulsory, they're steamy and hot.
Distance still kept, a yard and a half
No more close up, that makes you laugh.

Three months between haircuts, that is for me
But really the barber is charging a search fee.
Ladies, I'm sure, will rush in through the door
For hair sets and make ups, this they adore.

The clubs and the pubs welcome back friends
But how do they cope with all the new trends?
Don't stand too close, no drinks at the bar,
I think that is stretching a little too far.

Some businesses not opening, can't pay the rent,
Others find that their resources all spent.
A sad world we live in, it can't get much worse.
Let's go to the pub, I'm getting a thirst.

I Think

I sit and watch and even think
I'm told by doc, I'm in the pink
But many thoughts I have today
With many things that I could say

I think that I could sail away
Across the waters of the bay
Or climb the mountain in the west
Then be back, once more to rest

I think that I could even try
To fly a plane up in the sky
Or take a roller coaster ride
At least I can say that I had tried

I think that I must be getting old
Of all the things that I've been told
The things in life that I have seen
Seem nothing more than in a dream

I think that I'm entitled to
Just sit and think, as I like to do
To hell with all the worldly woe
Watch and think and let words flow.

It's a Bugger Getting Old

I recall, so many long years ago
When I could bend and touch my toe
Ride my bike, or go on a hike
I could do most anything I like

But times have changed, rust settles in
Just like it does on an unused hinge
The legs move slower, more aches and pain
I hanker for those young days again

The back is bent, the loads not light
To walk a ramp, I have to fight
The belt around my waist is tight
I tell you, friend, not a pretty sight

The eyesight dim, the hearing weak
Have trouble hearing people speak
The tummy roles, the heartburn comes
Have trouble with the shopping funds

There's a walker here and canes too
And helping arms on both our loo
A moving chair upon the stair
Considering all, I think that's fair

Ain't had a bath for many years
Getting out fills me with fears
There's worse to come, so I'm told
It's a bugger getting old.

It's a Walk in the Park

Went for a walk, down into the park
Walked through stalls, just for a lark
A sign at a stall, I must take a look
Words of wisdom, just like in a book

The words of wisdom filled me with glee
Here are the words, I'll share them with thee
I went to the psycho I knocked on her door
"Who was it there", she asked, in a bore

I left and went home, no more can I bear
People who asked, "Who was it there"
I continued my walk, perfume I smell
This is better, I can quickly tell

A sign on display, "this for the heel"
I replied to the lass, "I know how you feel"
Once, I too, was a bit of a cad
She looked so puzzled, I felt rather sad

I then gave a lesson on old Aussie slang
She seemed so surprised then her phone rang
I left her there cradling her phone
As I departed, she let out a groan

Once more I'm off, a doghouse I see
Asked him if there's room there for me
His wife then came in, her voice, she had lost
Best day for him and now he is the boss

Left him there with his hot dogs and wife
While I got on with living my life
Related the story when I got home
The outcome was then "no more will you roam".

It's Lifted

We hear the call, it's freedom day
But what's the price they'll have to pay
If they go out on a drinking spree
Then cases soar, we all agree

This delta strain, no cares nor fears
Sure to be around for many years
If in groups you wish to gather
Delta then can go "hell for leather"

Just because you're vaccinated
And you're fit and have been rated
Think of others who are not
The ones who won't have the shot

In this life of rush and hurry
How much time is put in worry?
You race on, in blinded haste
Too much of life is put to waste

So now that freedom day is here
Remember, friends, that life is dear
Celebrate, use life and wealth
For delta waits with bated breath.

It's Not a Race

Many's the time we've heard it said
Whether we're eating or going to bed
It's not a race, when we're getting a jab
Or that's what the Pollies have said

The figures are up, more covid is heard
We wait now for the magic word
It's not a race; we keep getting told
They'd better be quick, before I'm too old

Other countries have been given the jab
Many of them use the new word fab
We're in this together, another new phase
It's only the eyebrows that we see raised

It's not a race, I'm off for a walk
A mask on my face, so I don't get caught
The rest of the world is racing, I fear
Leaves us behind in the dust and the rear

The States are in turmoil, gone off the boil
Waiting around for the big boss's call
It's not a race, is the words that he uttered
The rest of us though, it's moan and muttered

In fifty years' time, if we're all still around
Pacing and racing all over the ground
Will the words keep ringing around in my mind?
It's not a race, is still with me, I find.

It's Not a War

In this year of twenty-two, I ask of you
What Russia is doing, is it true
Attacking Ukraine, it's not done before
But then they insist "it's not a war"

Planes fly over dropping bombs as they flow
Killing and maiming those thousands below
Trucks and tanks with men galore
Yet still they say "it's not a war"

Peace keeping soldiers are what they are
Ask any Russian, they know from afar
Women and children hurt and sore
Russia still saying "it's not a war"

Ukrainian men, and women too
Take up arms, as they should do
To fight their foe, as they've done before
To fight this fight "it's not a war"

Thousands of men and women die
To escape from this, women and children try
But Russia closes the escape door
With a frantic cry "it's not a war"

Towns and cities left in rubble heaps
The sight of "war" gives one the creeps
Still the battle goes on some more
Poor old Russia "it's not a war"

When war is over and peace restored
Proof handed to the war times board
What can the Russians say but more
Of their usual phrase "it's not a war".

It's Scary

I looked into the bathroom mirror
Was in for quite a fright
My hair was long and mattered
And my whiskers quite a sight

With some grease upon the hair line
And the part three inches wide
But the wrinkles on the forehead
We're the hardest ones to hide

So to the barbers, I am heading
For a quick cut, back and sides
And a little dash of lather
It's surprising what it hides

With the glasses fitting snugly
While the ears are using aids
And the skin shows weather damage
Shows the years that I have paid

But the many years I've suffered
All the good and all the bad
I've outlived my many school friends
And of this I'm very proud

But it's onward, up and onward
There's no time to play around
For I've much to do and conquer
Before they plant me in the ground.

I Wonder

I sit upon my thinking chair and wonder what will be
When I awoke this morning the sky looked like a sea
The clouds rolled like the oceans, breakers
    everywhere
A vicious wind was blowing, clouds racing here
    and there

A sprinkling of raindrops, down through the turbid air
Directed by the pressures of the air flow, which is
    there
Rain drops on my windowpane, falling fast and clear
Shame to have the window shut at this time of year

Lightning flashes overhead, thunder lets out a roar
Makes a noise and rattle on my old back door
Thor, God of thunder, seems really after me
Sending down his thunderbolts, just to frighten thee

He's had his little fun with me now he's on his way
Off to harass someone and have his little say
The rain has gone, it's cleared off with the thunder
There's little more to say, so I'll just sit and wonder.

Joseph

Is it Joseph, with his famous coat?
I ask you all to please take note.
I met this man in Tokyo
A city that is on the go.

He stood beneath a railway line.
I asked if he would mind
If I took his photo there
With coat, stick and his facial hair.

A wide smile and head he'd nod
Must have thought that I was odd.
There he stood, a picture great
I considered him a great mate.

With picture taken, I depart
Very pleased and very smart
Had to wait, it's like a dream
To get him on my T.V. screen.

Judgement Day

The judging is on, once more we'll see
Who the champion club will be
With biros out and glasses on
Reading writing by the ton

There's a good one here, I'll put it out
A beauty here, I hear him shout
No, too bordering, I'll put it aside
I've one here I should not hide

The poetry's done, we've judged the lot
Found ourselves a winning plot
The writing next, who'll be the next
I think I like this one the best

The judge for the photos, next in line
This is where the judge work is fine
Many shots to see this year
Some disappointment in the crowd, I fear

All judgement done, the winners named
It's all work top class, no one shamed
Who will wear the crown of fame?
It's Newcastle who won the crown, again.

Judith

Saddened is the world, we've lost one of our own
A girl who came from old Melbourne town
The joys they bought, her and the boys
With singing and music, Oh for the joys

A voice to be remembered for many years
All of your fans have shed many tears
You are among the best of the best
The voice of an angel is put down to rest

We will remember the tunes that you sang
Georgy Girl, that you sang with the band
Morningtown Ride and Wild Rover, for sure
I Am Australia, of which I adore

Rest now in peace, you've earned your rest
In this world you were the best
The words of your song are ever so true
We'll never find another you.

July Rains

The midday sky is dark and grey
No sign today of the sun at play
Rain falls down on sodden ground
Even the farmers watch and frown

For days the rains have tumbled down
Disaster and flooding all over town
Forecast says there's more to come
All we see is the damage done

Cars and people caught in the flood
SES to help, knee deep in mud
Trees and branches over roads
Volunteers there to shoulder loads

A month of rain in just three days
That's what the weather bureau says
Roads and houses under water
No rain relief from any quarter

Evacuations and rescues made
Hopes of sun so quickly fade
Down the track, we hope to see
A bright blue sky over a calm blue sea.

Kanahooker

Can a hooker be at rest
In our town, or just a pest
Or would our copper come and book'er
In our town of Kanahooker

Often I just sit and ponder
Or perhaps it's just I wonder
What would happen to this dame
If our town took on this fame

Wollongong, our closest city
Looks on us, as if in pity
But the men in our fair town
Takes it all with just a frown

Then our ladies, in their hurry
Hides their heads, as if in worry
Till they work out what to do
With this lass, named Lindy Lou

But it's a storm within a teacup
For there's been a great let up
She's moved on to greener pasture
After a word from our dear pastor.

Kanahooker Lass

Met a gal from Kanahooker
She was such a nifty looker
Light blonde hair, eyes of blue
Had a look of proud and true

Winked at me, as she passed by
Sure she tried to catch my eye
Dropped her hanky, nice and neat
Landed right on my big feet

A nice big smile, she gave me
As I kneel down on my bent knee
To retrieve for her, her little rag
To be returned to her handbag

But now, my friend, it's sad to say
As she moves out, on her way
My chances gone, of so it seems
As I wake up from one of my dreams.

Keep Ahead

I've heard it said and often read
Just quit when you're ahead
This advice I give to you
For my friend, it's very true

I saw this head just sitting there
It seems to me he's not a care
His pipes gone out, he doesn't worry
He's going nowhere in a hurry

I saw him on an ocean cruise
He's the one to make the news
Just sitting there, without a care
Meeting passengers who paid their fare

He is of the modern breed
Doesn't need to have a feed
Even though his hair's gone grey
Wouldn't have it any other way

Then to one and all, I say
Coming to the close of day
Don't lose temper or your head
Just keep in there and keep ahead.

Keep Dreaming

I remember the time, long, long ago
The Great Depression was still on the go
Workers on hold, left out in the cold
And Hitler, then not really so bold

I struggled at school, with the A B and C
And maths and the spelling of see
But the words from the mouth of mother dear
Was "keep dreaming" along there, don't fear

The Second World War put lives on the line
While I carried on with my junior school time
And struggle we did, as countries fall
But work, finally, was found for us all

I started work, on a leisurely course
As I joined the commonwealth force
Then later I spied a lovely young bride
And married the lass, with some pride

The words mother said rebound in my head
"Keep dreaming", my son, 'til you're dead.
I remember them well, to my son I now tell
"Keep dreaming" it comes as a yell.

My dreams have come true, as I come into view
Of Africa's magnificent, open air zoo
I've stood on the lip of Niagara Falls
"Keep dreaming", it comes as recalls

Taj Mahal, in its glory, a never-ending story
Greece and its Islands, I soak in its glory
Americas, I've seen North and South
Blame "Keep dreaming" I haven't a doubt

I've travelled the world, one-thirty or more
But who is it keeping the score
I'll go 'til I drop, I'll keep on the hop
Didn't learn the meaning of stop

But now in my nineties, it's never say die
I'd be off, in the flash of an eye.
I watch travel docs, while I'm streaming
But always remember "Keep Dreaming".

King Charles

There are things going on in the city
The Queen has died, such a pity
But now London's on show once more
For a replacement for Queen, that's the law

There's a King, whose been waiting for years
A chap that could bore you to tears
The Royals of the day says he stays
A coronation to be held within days

Millions have come for the show
To the city, it is really a glow
With red, white and blue to the fore
We couldn't ask for anything more

The best of the forces are there
Dressed out with the greatest of care
Horses and carriages too
Oh, what a great big "to do"

The moment has finally arrived
Charles, I'm sure he'll survive
The world's who's who are in place
With smiles or frowns on their face.

The king is crowned in the end
Now he has fences to mend
The sealing of all of this thing
A rendition of God save the king.

Koala

On top of the gum trees you'll see them there
Up in the tree top without a care
Curled up asleep, in the fork of a branch
Sleeping away, as if in a trance

Most of his day he lays in sleep
Opens his eyes when it's time to eat
No need to worry if the dingo's yap
He's safely away as he takes a nap

Trees rock to the tune of a gentle breeze
When the winds blow it's likely to freeze
Leaves and branches weave and float
He stays warm in his thick, furry coat

Seldom does he leave his tree-top home
For food and water, no need to roam
His gum tree home provide it all
He's contented, rolled up in a ball.

Land of Make Believe

I'm going off to somewhere, a land of make believe
Where our cares and worries, we find are soon relieved
A land of giant umbrellas, dancing with the breeze
If you do not like it, you can change it with a sneeze

Beyond a gentle river, there a crater can be seen
Painted bright with crystals, of red and gold and green
And if by chance you wander, across this special place
You'll meet up with a dragon, with a green and yellow face

If you are feeling thirsty, there's a fountain by your side
A handle there to help you, it's the best you've ever tried
Two maidens there to help you, treating you with care
Then lay back in comfort, on a bed of compressed air

Watching shooting stars in the rainbow-coloured sky
If you'd to try it, you'd see that you could fly
Up with the gentle monsters, and overseas of ice
Or down into canyons where you can play with mice

When the night is over and I get out of bed
Head towards the shower, my feet feel full of lead
I puzzle with my thinking, for I don't know where I've been
Then in shock and horror, I must have had a dream.

Leaves

With the coming of winter, the leaves start to fall
From the trees in the garden, the short and the tall
There's brown and green, and all in between
A carpet of colour, upon the grasses so green

The harshness of winter is there to be seen
Upon branches so bare, but once they were green
To heavens they reach, as if saying prayers
Standing alone, or sometimes in pairs

The winds play their magic, a dance they display
Moving the leaves, as if they're in play
Then overnight Jack Frost has put on a show
Upon the leaves, shrivelled and covered in snow

Soon we see magic, spring has arrived
Trees have awakened, and have survived
Green is the colour seen on the trees
Gently they sway in the afternoon breeze.

Lessons Learned

Across these lands that we call home
Be it New York, London, Rome
This scourge that's hit across our lands
Results are in World's leaders' hands

With the peoples of the Nation
Most of them in isolation
Many people stand agog
Seeing cities clear of smog

Less pollution, cleaner air
Makes it best for all who care
Cleaner seas and cleaner oceans
Helps the earth and tidal motions

Is this virus caused by pollution?
Or is feral meat the real solution?
When this virus is laid to rest
Who have learned the lessons best?

Life After

I awake from a cold, deep sleep
My body weight, no more I keep
A ring of angels, I see pass by
Across a sea of pink blue sky

I pause a while, adjust, I must
To take in sights of angel dust
A whirling trail of dust I see
This new awakening now for me

No sun I see, just an amazing scene
Like when I woke from an earthly dream
A light, so gentle, there to see
Pulsating there within what's me

No feelings there, yet feel I can
As gentle as a newborn lamb
No wind, no rain, just joy I be
Like an angel, I feel so free.

Life and Death

This earth of ours, once pristine clean
Skies so blue, grass so green
Rivers run down to the sea
Seas and oceans pollution free

Man then came upon the scene
Pollution left, where he had been
Open cuts across the land
Dust and dirt covers town

Nature then takes a hand,
Fires blaze across the land
Flood destruction, flooded towns
Destructive winds, wires down

Volcanos, quakes, tsunamis too
Panic then, what do they do?
Is it too late to start again?
Afraid the world is racked with pain

Men, we see, is slow to learn
For on their neighbour they do turn
With guns and bombs, mortar shells
Looks like we're on our way to hell.

Life is Hard

In isolation, here I sit
Hale and hearty, feeling fit
Upon the wall I see a fly
I use the spray and see it die

Life's very hectic, here at home
While, no more allowed to roam
I pull the pussy by the tail
And listen to the mournful wail

The budgie, in his gilded cage
Let out a squark, as if in rage
He seems to think that I was cruel
But I had only acted the fool

Time moves on, I've had my lunch
I still feel like something to munch
I'll have to raid the cookie jar
I don't think I've gone too far

My exercise has been such fun
Around the house I've had my run
Upstairs and down, I've done them all
Even had a gentle fall

It's time for me to go to bed
I must go and rest my head
When I rise and have been fed
I'll prepare myself for the day ahead.

Life is Murder

Once I was happy, life was a ball
Now I'm locked up, like a horse in a stall
I visit my doctor, she's in a rage
"I've told you before, it's because of your age"

No sympathy at all, it's the problems of life
I'd be in more trouble if I had a wife
Sail on I must, no quitting for me
I'll keep on droning like an old bumble bee

Eyes keep on watering, hearing not good,
Just keep on breathing, like everyone should
My meals are prepared and put on a plate
I just keep on wondering, what is my fate

I sit and I read or just watch the "box"
Don't have to comb my ex curly locks
It, like my life, is all in the past
We know from the start, things do not last

Life is murder, it's often been said
I'll keep on living, until I am dead
The Lord in the heavens knows what is best
For me, I just hope, that I am well blessed.

Life of Ned

Australian mountains, wide and vast
Hiding stories from our past
Bush rangers used them, by the score
I'll bring one story to the fore

Ned Kelly, with his brazen gang
Robbed many coaches in the land
Clad in coat of crafted steel
Bullets then, he didn't feel

In Glenrowan pub, he left his mark
The gang had gathered for a lark
Policeman there with weapons drawn
Had captured Ned Kelly, in pre-dawn

To Melbourne jail they took poor Ned
Tucked him up so tight in bed
Prepared the lad for judges' court
A legal battle then was fought

Protests then from friends of Ned
Still the court case went ahead
The judge's ruling then was read
Hang by the neck till you are dead

The last words that Ned Kelly said
"Such is life" before pronounced "dead"
Today in folk law many say
A harsh penalty he had to pay.

Life's Lottery

You picked a bad time to leave me, Doreen
My numbers came up on my screen.
The pools let me know, I'm rolling in dough,
Good times are now on the flow.

You know, how at night you would scream?
Well now my life runs like a dream.
No argue, no fight, I'm going alright
So everything shiny and bright.

Remember the bed that we used
The one hardly ever abused
Now stands in the shed, as a shrine
To show the passing of time.

The rest of your lot, from the wall
Is headed for Saint Vincent DePaul.
So sue if you like, I like a good fight
The best thing for you is take flight.

My address, no more with the slobs
I live up here with the snobs.
The sights and sounds are so clear
I live with a blonde in Belair.

Life's Quirks

Been through this world for ninety years
With happiness, joy and even tears
Then look back at things I've seen
And to the many places been

In decade one was fun and school
Didn't break the golden rule
Played the game as best I could
Just as I knew that I should

Finished school and off to work
Thinking life was just a perk
Soon found out it was not so
Then had to have another go

Married now and working harder
That's because I'm now a father
Boy and girl, just one of each
Life's come ripe, just like a peach

Now the forties loom before me
And my life is not so free
Work and home life to the fore
Don't have room for any more

The fifties brought a change to life
Separated from long-time wife
Kids married, left for their home
I was free to start to roam

Sixties, took a retirement plan
No more worries, no more ban
Found a friend and settled down
Moved and found another town

In this decade we made many plans
To see the world and use some rands
Africa, Europe the oceans too
Even saw Africa's natural zoo

The eighties saw no slack of speed
Travel books we'd sit and read
Slower was my walking pace
No plans on leaving the human race

With the nineties, still it's me
I'm still sailing upon the sea
But my thoughts seem to go
Towards that big one, the double O.

Life's Road

Along this road of life we travel
Sometime smooth, but often gravel
We travel on, as best we can
Yet wonder where this life began

We've travelled far throughout this life
Some with husband, others with wife
And children, too, along the way
But now the hair is turning grey

We look back on those early days
Our mums and dads would have their says
Right or wrong, we must obey
That's the game we had to play

Through this life of stress and worry
Always seem to be in a hurry
Haven't time to smell the flowers
Looking for the strength and powers

Then, at last we're out to pasture
Where our time is moving faster
But our time is all our own
Together with our aches and groans

Sitting there upon an armchair
Often now without a care
Waiting for our time to go
But just to where? We do not know.

Life's Time

Don't weep for me, for I am so old
Seen most of the world, many stories told
Life has been good, health has been fair
What's up ahead, I'll just have to bear

I look back on life and what I have been
Started school young and ended in teens
Worked all my life in the Government field
Retirement came, my work life was sealed

Wondered now just what I should do
I fell for the wonders of travel, and knew
The world is a big place, with much to see
Relax on a ship as it sails over the sea

Travelled to Paris and saw the Eiffel tower
Tried to climb it, but I'd run out of power
Next off to Barcelona, to see their great church
Then to the bank, to replenish my purse

But sailing, for me, is the best way to go
Just get on the ship and go with the flow
I've sailed all oceans and most of the seas
And now I sit back and do as I please

As I have said, don't be sorry for me
I find that age is but a number, you see
So I'll carry on, just one day at a time
And lap up the sun, just let it shine.

Lights

It's New Year's Eve in the city
Everything at night looks so pretty
The city's alive with magical lights
Around it, the best of the sights

The colours, against the black night
A pleasure for anyone's sight
Exploding in air, with the greatest of care
The magic of thought and of flare

The colours of red, blue and green
Through smoke haze are easily seen
The viewers on shore let out a great roar
As explosions are heard door to door

The Bridge soon comes into view
Decked out in radiant blue
A tribute to nurses, and staff
They worked from daylight to dark

From the boats in the harbour we see
More rockets heading for sea
Ten minutes of light, it's gone in a flash
With thousands enjoying the bash.

Lockdown

The walls needed painting, shutters a clean
I must get around to it, that's what I mean
Glass doors and windows, a clean is a must
Cracks in the doors admit lots of dust

The garden, a jungle, weeds everywhere
We watered the garden, attended with care
The lawn that we had, now a garden of weeds
Galahs and corellas feed on the seeds

Letter box needs replacing, but we get little mail
I was thinking of putting the house up for sale
But now we are in lockdown, time on my hand
May order compost, and a half ton of sand

I wake of a morning, great plans in my mind
Head for my breakfast, my mind in a bind
Switch on the Tele, see how Delta preformed
Stay home in isolation, is what I've been warned

Can't go and buy paint, stay at home they do tell
Shops are not open, they have nothing to sell
I look at the garden, they're set in their bed
I'll go back inside, like the Premier has said.

Lost in Scotland – Part 1

Miriam and Alan, a likely pair
Off in a motor home, oh what a scare
Over Bloody Eighty, still not a care
Wheelchair in tow, oh what a pair

Alan the artist, of many years
Quite the performer, from what one hears
Alan the chauffeur, Miriam the boss
Watch out Scotland, you're in for a loss

Into the van, Alan's hands on her bum
In it together, for he is her chum
Off to see where her father had lived
With family together, when they were just kids

Off to the castle, is Alan the King
No, not the right genes, that is the thing
Now to the house where he once stayed
Not happy then, not happy these days

A stop at a mill, made a tartan for me
A toilet seat cover as bright as can be
Back in the van, a trip to the loo
A camera above is looking on too

At the castle of Cawdor, we walk down the hall
Alan's look alike painting, hung on the wall
Met with The Lady, so full of grace
We lingered there, there was no need of pace

At Fordyce I met with a ghost from the past
Young Billy Patterson, he's one of the last
Forty years ago, we played in our role
Today we're too old and out in the cold.

Lost in Scotland – Part 2

Off to Ullapool we leisurely go
The town laid out as if on show
While Alan sails around the bay
I learn how to make midges pay

Alan learns to sail round the lake
I've mixed and matched the midge's fate
Learned about the men's jock strap
How they're kept and nicely wrapped

To watercolour studio, where Alan sang
While I spent time with goats and ram
Pat and brush their lovely coat
But which of us is the biggest goat

Back to the van to visit Glencoe
A terrible sight of chair lift and snow
Took the cowards way out, went up by car
The easiest way to get there, by far

The trouble with ageing, it creeps up on you
No body warns you, this I find true
And the view from the top, is worth it, I fear
While I'm getting older, year after year

No rest for the wicked, or those getting old
The wheels moving faster, and I'm feeling bold
Inverness next, to this magical city
Not here for long, that is the pity

Ding dong, calls the witch, by the bell
Into the coven, with much more to tell
Got arrested for parking on a double yellow line
Told the cop, his dick is so small, result is a fine

We end this leg with a song and a drink
Covered a lot, this time I think
The scenery we've seen, a treasure to behold
Worth its weight in a nugget of gold.

Lost In Scotland – Part 3

Lost in Scotland, but heading south
Rain is falling and I'm using my mouth
To Dingwall to see haggis being made
Alan in the sun while I'm in the shade

Monifieth we motor, for a golfing lesson
The coach, in high voice, we'll take no messing
He showed me the way that I must play
But my left tit kept getting into the way

For breakfast, we head into the farms
Where I have a cucumber, firm in my palms
Fresh onions are prepared for us to eat
Hope there's not people that we have to meet

Some beautiful country, with clouds in the sky
For this country, they'd willingly die
The haggis we made, Alan's was long
While mine was short and a little strong

Off to Edinburgh, the city of lights
Many people and many delights
Must leave this city, we're heading off home
I wonder, once more, if together we'll roam.

Lost Weekend

He was tall, dark and handsome
With a blonde upon his arm
They walked into a jeweller's shop
Their faces full of charm

The jeweller races over to assist
A most expensive ring and necklace
Is the request that's made to him
Forty thousand dollars, nothing less

The jeweller rubs his hands with glee
A cheque will be the payment for the ring
Knowing three days will be required to clear
The man and blonde exit, with a grin

On the following Monday, man received a call
The cheque was rejected, out of cash.
He was humble as he answered to the man
The weekend had been great but purchase rash.

I've just had a weekend I'll never forget
But tear up the cheque and throw it away
I don't need the promise of jewels any more
It takes way too much effort for that kind of play.

Lunch, Cocky Style

In the wee small hours in our kitchen room
We keep it tidy with vacuum and broom
But what a surprise when I put on the light
I couldn't believe what I had in sight.

A cockroach was there, with table and chair
Awaiting the arrival of another cock pair.
The table was set with cockroach food
Awaiting arrivals and to get into the mood.

The sight of the light, scared him away
But soon he was up and ready to play.
As I moved around, he watched what I did.
He crawled under a cupboard, there just hid.

I chased after him, my slipper in hand.
I kept watching to see where he'd land.
His movements were quick, I landed a whack
Splattered that cocky, with him on his back.

Maxi Mum

When I was a baby, on my mother's knee
She clothed and fed and nourished me
Always there when I tried to walk
Guided me when I tried to talk

Read stories to me and older brother
Showed herself the perfect mother
Put our cares before her own
So we can show respect, when grown

Off to school, it's hand in hand
She became my greatest fan
Taught me to know right from wrong
Handled matters all day long

There to tend my aches and pains
And to help out with my claims
She's on duty night and day
Wouldn't have it any other way

Added five more children to her flock
No more working by the clock
Night and morning, and in between
She became the family "queen"

Left home now to make my life
Found its time to take a wife
Work and family, I struggle on
But don't forget my dear old mum

Her life rolls on, it's time to rest
The body is worn and past its best
A message out to one and all
The time has come, the curtains fall

There she lay, in a hospital bed
White and still, as if she's dead
The Lord took her to His breast
I've lost mother, friend, she was the best.

Miriam

Alice Springs, is the real living heart
Central Australia, playing its part
North or south, east or west
Right in the middle, it is the best

Met with the indigenous Alice Springs mob
Laughed and played, as they did their job
Shocked at the way they have to live
With stories and legion, they have lots to give

To Daly Waters, just a one-horse town
Arrived in town, with the sun going down
Met there a man, just as large as life
Runs the town with the help of his wife

In Darwin's fair city, more sights are seen
The water in harbour so blue and so clean
Met with transvestites and lesbians galore
A night at the club was just what you adore

Two weeks in this city, life is a great feast
You're leaving here now, heading off east
To visit a mine, and talk with the head male
And to see where miners live, a glorified jail

Then get caught up in a rally, they call it a bash
All drivers are cheerful, there's no need for a clash
There're colours and costumes and cars dressed too
You even made use of their portable loo

Turn to the south, it's the Gold Coast you seek
Looks like you'll stay there, at least for a week
With nippers and strangers, you're having some fun
Just walking and roaming around in the sun

Then heading off south, through cities and towns
On roads made for travel, homewards you're bound
You pass on from Sydney and on down the coast
You're sure you're an Aussie, or that is your boast

The journey is over, many sights you have seen
The good, the bad, the ugly, the mean
You've seen Australia, and now you can be
As warm, and lovely and an Aussie, like me.

Miriam Margolyes (The Australian)

She came from Robertson to Sydney, to see
If Aussies were warm and living so free
Went to Paddy's market, to purchase some eats
This lady renowned for so many feats

Went to "The Hills" to view a nice home
But if she bought it, no more would she roam
Once a Pom, but an Aussie she became
To bathe in the glory of the great Aussie fame

Then over the ranges, to Orange she sped
For a day and a night, but the town was quite dead
On then to Trundle, she went, full of grace
To see this small town, of a much slower pace

You've seen for yourself, the drought and the dust
With grass and paddocks the colour of rust
But with rain and the sun, the colours you'll see
Will fix shattered lives and fill you with glee

Then off to Melbourne, you motored all day
Went into Vinnies for a jacket, they say
There you got talking to an Afghani lad
He talked of his troubles and the loss of his dad

With Melbourne behind you, then headed for Nhill
The country so lush, over valley and hill
Meets up with a family and stays on for tea
And marvels at new Aussies and what they can be

From Adelaide we head off directly north
Road straight and flat, no changes in course
For scenery, I'm afraid, there's not much to see
Just dirt and dust and the occasional tree

That night you stayed at a roadside stop
With truckies, campers, you had the lot
Had a ride on a large interstate road-train
Looked to the skies, no sign there of rain

Mate is a word used by Aussies most
A common word, used coast to coast
A word meaning more than just a plain friend
It's mate, a person on who you can depend.

Mischief

I have a brand-new little kitten
And mischief is his name
He is Black and Tan and cheeky
And mischief is his fame

I've tried to potty train him
And feed him from a tin
Of all the things that I have tried
You would think they were a sin

I'd sit and watch him wriggle
While playing in the sun
But then off chasing butterflies
He thinks that it is fun

I try to use some magic
To get him to take heed
But the only things of interest
Is playing and his feed

Then when I really scold him
He rolls up into a ball
And looks at me so pleadingly
I'm the one to take the fall

But this tiny little kitten
So small and yet so cute
Is happy in my lounge room
This I can't refute.

M is for Mother

M is for mother, a sweet, loving lady
One who takes care of her little baby,
Nurtures and nourish and tenderly cares
Whether they come single, or even in pairs

The time and devotion for her little joy
A lovely little girl or big bouncing boy
The loving's the same whichever arrives
She gives of her best, whatever she tries

As baby progresses, her care's still the same
To give baby the best, is her cherished aim
To teach and protect and cuddle some more
For life with a baby is never a bore

The years carry on, he's ready for learning
He's off to school while mums at home yearning
The day is so long while they are apart
For his days at school are only a start

After the years of schooling he's had
With mother behind him, it's not been too bad
Onto the dais, with diploma in hand
Mum is so proud of her wonderful man

A daughter in law, she accepts with some pride
Who stands with her son, side by side
Soon there's to be a new little bairn
So mum can start mothering all over again.

Missed a Bit

I am a single lady
Living by myself
My parents often told me
I'd be left upon the shelf

With the coming on of Spring
I have lots of work to do
Clean the tiles and carpet
And then the chimney flue

Then I see my windows
There're dirt and dust and goo
I do not have a ladder
But know what I will do

I opened up my directory
A window cleaner, I did see
I rang him up immediately
Said, he'll come to see me

The work is finally over
He told me of the cost
Then when I went to pay him
My mind was at a loss

He took the money eagerly
Then said he's missed a bit
I looked at him, in terror
Then explained, he's Mr. Bit.

Morning

I stand upon the ocean cliff, my cane within my hand
The sun just peeping over water, just as I had planned
The early rays of morning light, around the edges fold
While on the water etches the early shades of gold

As the sun creeps upward, the colours come alive
Across the waveless ocean, the sun rays slowly drive
Showing ships at anchor, awaiting their berth time
The sun has cleared the horizon, ready now to shine

The seagulls sing a welcome, another day begun
A welcome to the world, by the early morning sun
A gentle zephyr blowing, across the sea of blue
The sun is headed upward, along a path so true

Our land casts off its shadows, revealing that below
The sun soon hurries onward, a million miles to go
A land of rugged beauty, bathed in morning light
While our busy farmers, begin their daily fight

Morning turns to evening, another day has passed
The sun, across the heavens, its rays asleep at last
A silvery moon is shining, announcing night is here
With darkness overtaking, soon morning will
    reappear.

Morning Time

I hear the gentle rustle of the leaves beneath the trees
An early summer morning, sends along a pleasant breeze
The sun is peeping through a slightly cloudy sky
Birds are up early, through the trees they quickly fly

Nature, in it's wisdom, sends many sights along
If you don't accept them, soon they will be gone
Just take in the beauty of the things we see around
Whether in the airways, or deeply in the ground

Days are long and lonely, if you just pass them by
Take in the things around you, be they walk or be they fly
Consider all your options, as you pass on through this life
Look at all the beauty, forget the way of strife

This world has been around a million years and more
Sharing out it's beauty, from the sky back to the shore
The sun has risen higher, to show the world around
Take in all that's offered, before you're underground.

Mother's Joy

Joey arrived, not yet covered in hair
Just how much more can a mother bare
Than a joey in pouch, making a mess
All that she wants, is just take a rest

The dads been around, no interest he takes
Soon hops off, no comment, he makes
It's mother, alone, to tend to the son
While dads off having kangaroo fun

The onus is on her, to teach her young
To be quiet when she's on the run
A bumpy old road, he's to endure
With bumps and bashes he may be sore

A matter of months, he views the outside
The jump from the pouch, this he has tried
Got caught up with tail and long legs
Help me out mum, this he begs

Soon he is out and off with the pack
Others there to take up the slack
Mother will watch him, as he makes his way
Contented to watch, as with others he'll stay.

Mummy and Paddington

Mummy and Paddington off to the fair
Hurry, we must, lots will be there
A front seat for us, that goes without saying
You had better be quick, we won't be staying

They're here to see the jubilee celebrations
The first to be held in any of nations
Seventy years in one occupation
This really is a great dedication

Back to the palace they quickly went
Mummy is tired, energy all spent
A marmalade sandwich, we have to eat
With a nice cup of tea, that you can't beat.

Murrumbidgee River

From the Monaro Plains it heads out west
Through the country, some of the best
Starting its rush from near Cooma town
Out through the west, heading right down

Through village and towns this river flows
On fields and valleys, where the wind blows
Watering fields and stock, on its way down
Providing water for these country towns

Fishing and boating, this river's the one
Swimming or fishing, it's a river for fun
The city of Wagga is soon seen and past
It's said of this river, the volume is vast

The Lachlan joins in, to add to the flow
When rivers swell you should see it go
Onward they rush, until the Darling, they see
Then all waters flow out to the sea.

My Barber's Fee

My hair needs cutting, she says to me
Yesterday it's off to the barber to see
Back in the days, when only a lad
A trip to the barbers was not so bad

Remembering those days, I'd pay six pence
But a haircut I got, for it was so dense
Even so young it grew so well
Remembering to go after the school bell

So yesterday, I'm sitting in the barber's chair
Feeling him clip my remaining grey hair
Even though he scraped and hollowed
Eventually said, that's twenty-five dollars.

My Bike

I've had it since new, I'm telling you
Its colour is red with a smidgen of blue
When I'm out for a drink with my mate
I make sure that I've locked up the gate
My mate and I are eager to see
What the outcome of this could be
I'm sure it'll be fine, with the passing of time
I've been following this for a sign
The information is fine, when it came
I assure you, my friend, it's no game
Try as I might, through day and through night
I'll carry on with this fight
So back to the gate, I hike
To look at my red and blue bike.

My Christmas

My Christmas was good, you could say
I wouldn't have it any other way
Went down the coast with a friend
Nearly drove me quite around the bend

The road was uncrowned this year
She drove while I clung on in fear
No worries, we got there in the end
Caught up with a very old friend

The talks of Lord Howe Island, I fear
They go there regularly each year
They spent time at the bowling club bar
For while there they rent out a car

Ham and chicken with vegies for lunch
Washed down with a bottle of punch
Boiled pudding with custard was great
But afraid, served a little bit late

Bob had his usual old grouch
As I relaxed and sat on the couch
Dianne and Lyn, as a pair
Washes dirty dishes with care

We left for home around three
After leaving presents under the tree
The road coming home was a wonder
As I spent most of my time in slumber

It's gone and it's over, I fear
At least till the end of the year
If God in his wisdom, takes care
I'll be back if the world treats me fair.

My Colonoscopy

The surgery ward, they take me to
Because my body is feeling blue
Upon my nose, a tube is placed
Let's get it over, I think, in haste

I'm on my side, and neatly trussed
The surgeon then, I've put my trust
A flasher then is much like me
My bum is bare for all to see

I'm half asleep, not fully out
I feel the plunge but cannot shout
There's things inside, of this I'm sure
They poke about, I feel so sore

I think they have a herd of sheep
Walking around on tender feet
In the depths within my bowel
It's enough to make a grown man howl

The recovery room is next I see
All looks fine, except for me
A lady there with horns, I tell
Oh, Lord above, I've gone to hell

Ten minutes more, or so it seems
I've returned from the land of dreams
Dressed and clothed, no more in shame
And I've returned to the land of fame.

My Day Out

She took me out on a shopping spree
Many people there to see
Shops were open, people there
Hardly a vacant spot to spare

The deli was my first stop call
Where the staff are on the ball
I saw a tray of breasts, so bare
Remarked to the lass standing there

I like your breast, you have on show
In no uncertain manner said "you better go"
I hurried off, without my breast
Carried on, my thoughts the best

Another isle, a big sign said
Try our new, sliced loaf of bread
But when I opened it up to try
I got the look of the evil eye

A barrel full of fruit, I saw
This is what I'm looking for
The sign, it said, the fruit is free
But beneath the sign, I didn't see

In letters small, for kids it read
I helped myself, then my face went red
It was pointed out, but I hadn't seen
That bottom line, made me feel so mean

She said that its time that I must go
And moved me off, so very slow
Took me home then said "stay"
For me it's been such an exciting day.

My Elderly Friend

I saw her quietly sitting there
Rocking gently in an old rocking chair
The hair was thin and turning grey
A breeze had blown a few strands astray

The face looks pale, with lines shown
Perhaps with thoughts of children grown
A tear upon a well-worn face
With life now, there is no pace

The eyes now open, a smile appears
A life soon ends, there is no tears
The happy days that she once knew
Are with her husband, in yonder blue

Racked with pain, it can be seen
Twists and turns where arthritis been
The time is near, you'll hear the chord
To take you home, with Him, the Lord.

My Electrician

I tell a story, it's short and it's true
It happened to a friend that I knew
An electrician quoted a week for the works
But ended up doing a few of his perks

A week after he started, no end was in sight
My friend ended up with a terrible fright
He told her of Richard, who he'd taken with him
Wouldn't get up and work, it's really a sin

Two weeks on the job, with nothing to see
What's wrong with this man, what's it to be
He's racing around, more stock he must buy
Won't finish this job, but I wish he would try

Three weeks later, it's a day off for court
His Ex is suing, oh how hard she fought
Back on the job, with Richard so slow
How long will it take, how long now to go

Five weeks it took, then I gave him "go"
Like a cur he left, with Richard in tow
The work that he did, is good, I must say
But, oh, what a pile that I had to pay.

My E-mails

I was told I had some e-mails
But they hadn't come on through
They have been sent by neighbours
So what they say is true

But there's a hole down in my garden
And they seem to end up there
The climb up to my computer
Is a track that's only fair

So if you happen by my house
There's something you can do
Get out of your motor car
And help to push them through

But if I send out answers
It's as easy as can be
For when I send an answer
It's all downhill, you see

So if I haven't sent an answer
To stuff you've sent on to me
Don't blame the poor old postie
It's this new-fangled life, you see.

My Fly

I think I just saw a fly, yes, I did, I saw a fly
He gave a little buzz, just as he flew by
A very friendly fly, the apple of his mother's eye
He's on the lookout for a friendly guy

If he lands on you, don't you be bad
Welcome him and make him proud
A kiss from him and off he goes
Could land then on someone's toes

A friendlier guy you're yet to meet
You and he, you could not beat
But if you send him on his way
He'll be back to make you pay.

My Garden

I have in my garden, a lizard or two
Would you believe it, I ask of you
Night and day, they sit there and stare
Don't get too close, they're likely to glare

They've been there a while; I guess you can see
Not worried by flies or the odd honeybee
Just like a statue, they stand in the sun
While others around them are having fun

The garden looks fine, my gardener said
But the look of the lizards, looks like they're dead
Yet the people around, come in to stare
At the sight of the lizards, while ever they're there.

My Knight

I lay in bed and wonder
At the footsteps that I hear
And I pull the blankets closer
As I tremble in my fear

The footsteps are getting closer
I can hear them on the stair
Is it the reaper come to get me
For the sins that I must bare

Are my thoughts just over-acting
Or is there really something there
As I puzzle for an answer
I move with worried care

My heart is really pounding
And I worry what to do
Is it real or just imagination
Or is it just my dose of flu

As the seconds turn to minutes
I'm no clearer in my mind
Do I rise and challenge it
Or am I frightened what I'll find

In my state of nearly panic
There's a shining light I see
The room is bathed in brightness
It's my love that's come to me.

My Life

I look down on the land below
Carried on by the winds that blow
There's times that I am out of sight
Mostly in the dark of night

I travel round the world, you see
Over land and over sea
There's nothing here to hinder me
I'm as contented as I can be

When the moon is at full glow
Below the stars, I silently flow
Dressed in a skirt of brilliant white
Can be seen in bright sunlight

My place in life is for all to see
Black clouds appear, they worry me
Thunder and lightning fly fast by
Frighten me and make me cry

When the sun comes out again
Land below washed by rain
You will recall me, if you try
I'm the little white cloud that cried.

My Maiden Flight

A flight in the sky, I thought I'd try
My hands are sweaty and mouth is dry
My passport, visa and ticket handy
Been to the bar for an early brandy

Our flight is called, I move in fear
All seems right but a ring in the ear
A toilet stop, it should have been
But I was too busy watching a screen

Through the barrier, we're moving fast
If I don't hurry, I could end up last
Into the plane, I feel it shake
I'm starting to think, this is a mistake

Into my seat, I find at last
Many passengers moving past
The doors have closed, I'm locked in
I need a fag from tobacco tin

The planes in flight, I must settle down
I see tiny houses back down in town
I'm buckled in, I sit and pray
There's nothing more for me to say

I've settled down, trying to sleep
Soon I find, I'm counting sheep
Until I heard someone in pain
The wings come off the aeroplane

Panic, panic, I wake in fright
Goodness, gracious, what a sight
An aeroplane without a wing
I'd never heard of such a thing.

My Morning Walk

Along the lake, I went for a walk
Many like me, so I stopped for a talk
The topic for most, on everyone's lips
To lose weight from body and hips

But some show concern for the virus flu
Saying they're not sure what they should do
Just to continue, living day by day
To wait and see what the medicos say

Carrying on, there's more things in sight
A pair of black crows locked into a fight
Young lady runs past, as if her life is in danger
While I watch the antics of the council ranger

A lady passes with three young in a stroller
The look on her face looks colder and bolder
Then laughter from me, as I sip from my mug
Was dog in a stroller, wrapped up in a rug

It's pleasant to see, as I walk by the lake
A boat at mooring, its rope laid out like a snake
With never a ripple on the water so blue
Then Pelicans take off, over the water they flew

I struggle off home, my activities are done
Locked up again, shoes off and hat hung
Twenty-four hours and I'll do it again
Fresh air and walking and live with the pain.

My MPs

Of politics, I've had my fill
The same old stuff is with us still
They promise this, they promise that
I feel they're talking through their hat

The taxes, they still take from me
Though I've just turned ninety-three
Leave it with me, I'll get it done
I'll probably wait until I've turned a tun

The honest ones lay underground
That's the thing that I have found
In my time I've met a lot
All in all, they've lost the plot

Men and women, in tinsel town
Make the law then lay it down
Just for you and me, I'm sure
They're off flying, yes, offshore.

My Mutt

Just look at my mutt, asleep at my feet
Snoring so loud, like regular heartbeat
Curled up in a ball, his usual pose
A typical dog life, is what I suppose

When I rattle my keys, he's instantly awake
Wanting a ride, as I go for a steak
He waits at the door, a smile on his face
If only I had his life and his grace

Off to the butchers, I make a good pace
A bone in the offing, more smiles on his face
More shopping, I do, no interest he shows
His bone in the car, is all that he knows

A stranger approaches, too close, he has got
A snarl from the mutt, and the stranger is off
I arrive at the car, his tail wagging fast
Tries to tell me of things that has passed

Arriving back home, he's off like a shot
Back on his rug, the weathers too hot
I emptied my carload, it all looks so boring
But what of the mutt, I can hear he is snoring.

My Neighbour

She lives with her hubby in unit number one
A lass that we know, loves to have fun
Loves to visit with her beautician too
Just to fill in time, or she will feel blue

Her love is divided into just two
Holly, the dog and husband so true
The dog has the run of home, I am told
Cuddles up close when she feels the cold

The husband, a bowler, it's his kind of fun
But only when his housework is done
She's like the sun, warm and so bright
Not the type that looks for a fight

A smile and a word, as I wander past
From Holly a bark, as she moves so fast
I've known this lady for quite a long time
I'm pleased that she is a neighbour of mine.

My Nightmare

The thing that I dread, when I go to bed
Are things that happen within my head.
The dreams that occur make me fair curse
But of the nightmares, they really are worse

Last night, in my dream, I'm in a tour bus
It stops to alight, I push through the crush
The door is too small, I cannot get through
I go for the escape hatch, it's covered in glue

I tremble in panic, just what can I do
If I smash through the glass, then they will sue
The crowds getting noisy, they want to get out
I'm like a big jelly, but can't get about

The spell, quickly broken, I wake up in fright
Sheets twisted up, what a bad sight
A coffee for me, to settle me down
Then sit at the window, overlooking town

Tonight, in the dark, when I go to bed
I won't catch the bus, if my way it fled
I'll just lay back, let my life flow
And ride the nightmare, if it has to show.

My Pet

I have a little rabbit, I keep him in a hutch
Only feed him once a day, he don't eat too much
I let him out on Sunday, when I have time to play
I chase him round the garden, I think I'll let him stay

There's a big bird flying, up in the blue sky
I'll have to watch him closely, he's my rabbit in his eye
A big stick, I am waving, at that bird above
For my little rabbit, I have lots of love

I'll have to find a female for my furry friend
She could give him comfort, when I have things to tend
If they act like rabbits, then many more there'll be
Then I could open up, my own rabbit nursery

Ten thousand, saw I, at a glance, no, not a daffodil
But tiny little rabbits running round the hill
On second thoughts, perhaps I shouldn't get her in
And keep my little rabbit free from lust and from sin.

My Ps and Qs

I have to watch my P's and Q's
And watch the things that people use
I went to have a blood test done
Also knew it would not be much fun

Formed a Q, and with my P
Found the girl I was to see
But to my horror, I found out
It was my fast it's all about

Told to go home and sleep all night
Come back tomorrow, it would be alright
Next day I'm back with P and Q
Only to find out something new

Went to put the needle in, stopped and said
"What's this mark", I just shook my head
It was where I'd just had a CT done
Home you go again, my son

Another Ninety hours I had to wait
Until I'd know my final fate
So once again, with Q's and P
I'd front again, oh woe is me

My fate, this time, it's clear to see
Just what they have in mind for me
A jab, and then the blood would flow
Won't let them have a second go.

My Rear Window

I sit in a darkened hospital ward
The only one I can afford
A window there so large and bright
But looking out, Oh what a sight

No sign of oceans, seas or like
But large brick building, painted white
Iron grills upon the walls
To keep them in, or stop their falls?

Cracks appear upon the wall
Perhaps it's heading for a fall
If it falls, won't worry me
I'm twenty feet away, you see

The sun is shining, that's a plus
No use making such a fuss
We're here today and gone tomorrow
Leaving behind all grief and sorrow

Now my windows dark and brown
Night has come, sun gone down
Shutters down across the way
At least my friend, I've had my day.

My Shirt

She sits upon her balcony, like an eagle in her nest
Looks around the area, just to see who she can pest
Then eyes wide open, she has spotted her next fight
With her trusty camera, she has taken off in flight

Down the stairs, into the courtyard, before the
    image flees
Takes a photo of the hanging, of a shirt, if you please
Then back into her eyrie, she travels very fast
To snare another victim, this won't be her last

An e-mail she dispatches, to the owner of the shirt
Then puts in a little twist, just to make it hurt
But in her anxious hurry, she has made a grave
    mistake
She's claimed it's hanging on someone else's gate

Oh the horror of the story, as the e-mails come and go
And you get the feeling, is there something you
    could throw
Then you advise the writer of her typo in the text
She sends me then "I'm sorry" but I guess she's
    really vexed.

The story isn't ended, I'm sure there's more to come
It's being very petty, is being thought by some
It doesn't really matter, it's filling in her day
For it's the only way, that she can have her say.

My Steam Train

A grunt and a groan, it lets off a blast
An old steam engine, out of the past
With water and coal making the steam
Kids who see it, think it's all a big dream

Restored and repaired, it's ready to roll
Down the rail tracks, you'd better take hold
It's battered and worn, but a good head of steam
Along past paddocks and over the stream

A fireman there, to shovel the coal
The driver sights out through a large hole
The smoke above, left far behind
The wheels clop, clop right down the line

Train watchers watch on with such glee
The train taking off, as if it were free
Cows in the paddock panic and flee
The train just shows what it can be

Tomorrow we find it back in the shed
No more we see smoke from its head
Long is my memory of when a young boy
My train set, I had, was my favourite toy.

My Swift

Across the Hunter's roadway, along the Hunter's streets
A white Suzuki Swift has been going around for weeks
The driver, ever watchful, and looking where to turn
Her foot upon the pedal, she'll make this motor burn

The mind is ticking over, a poem will soon appear
She's pulled into a side street and turned it down a gear
With pen and paper handy, she'll write the wording down
Then scratch her head in wonder, upon her brow, a frown

A police car, on the lookout, sees her sitting there
Pulled up behind the motor, she is unaware
Any problems lady, he asks, with worried frown
She looks up in amazement and turns the window down

Just writing up a story, she answered to the cop
Your keys are in the ignition and you are in a stop
I'll have to write a story, a happy ending it won't be
An infringement I will make it, you will pay a fee

Soon the motor started, she, now homeward bound
But oh, which direction, I've lost round this town
Around and round for hours, I must be somewhere near
I'm covered now in lather and setting in with fear

Why don't they have a system and show me where to go
I seem forever driving by just going with the flow
Now I'm on the home stretch, my home is now in sight
I'll be on the road tomorrow for yet another bight.

My Time

Don't take me yet, I ask you Lord
I've books to read, their numbers soared
Many shows I've yet to see
Before I return to be with thee

Although I've crossed the line at times
I always think of things Devine
And do the things that I think right
While with the devil, I do fight

I'll hurry on and read some more
In case you enter through my door
But if perchance you let me stay
I'll be so good and even prey

At night, in bed, I often wonder
Particularly in the lights and thunder
Is this a warning, I should heed
Or stay in bed with a book to read

But in the end I know you'll call
For I'm not here for a lengthy haul
The time I've had I treasure thus
I'll go along without a fuss.

My Troubles

I have a little trouble, when my mind is not in gear
It seems to go off somewhere, it really is so queer
But if I think about it, it makes no sense at all
I think I'll rest awhile, and curl up in a ball

I can't think where I was, before I took a break
So think I'll start again, when first I was awake
This world of ours is moving, I can't keep up the pace
All this because I'm living in a different kind of race

I find that with the worry, of keeping a normal mind
The pace of modern living, has me in a bind
But battle on regardless, for I know not what's ahead
Then if all forsakes me, I can always go to bed

It's not that I'm a quitter, or cannot do the miles
But in this mind of mine, there ain't no room for files
So if you'll forgive me, and treat me very nice
I'll just sit here in the corner, and be as quiet as the mice.

My Visit

Along the hospital halls, I walked
People hurrying but no one talked
I stopped to ask directions there
From a young lady with long blonde hair

My question raised, she looked at me
With tattoos there for all to see
I'm sorry, sir, I can't quite say
For I am going the other way

With gurneys, crates and other stuff
My passage here proved quite ruff
I battled on and soon I found
A lady there to guide me round

Soon I'm sitting in a waiting room
There's a cleaner with a great big broom
But sit I must, for my turn to come
Finally they called "you're the one"

In a darkened office, there I go
Looks at my foot and my big toe
Writes out a script then says "be off"
And take care of that nasty cough

Back through those halls of fame I go
Into my car, the petrol's low
Up to the garage, fill her up
Then off home for a good hot cup.

Nan's Escape

N is for Nan, happy as a lark
But found by police, lost in the park
Home to her daughter, grounded again
For being at home was really a pain

Filled her suitcase with dozens of spuds,
Then picked flowers, just into buds
Donned her overcoat, stood by the door
Off home to England she's heading once more

They realized by this, she was losing the plot
Decided to find her a nursing home slot
Off to the mountains, Leura in fact
Nicely dressed and her suitcase all packed

Freedom at home, was her daughter's thought
For mum was placed in a home, like a fort
With fences, locked gates and security guard
To escape from here would be very hard

Three months there, before the escape
Someone had left a wide-open gate
Out like a shot and down to the rail
No one following, left them not trail

On to the train and heading for home
Nothing with her, not even a comb
On to the platform, a snapper was there
He murmured, pool lady, this isn't fair

Back to the village, by police, in their car
It won't be too long, but it really is far
The daughter was told of the daring escape
They locked nan inside and bolted the gate.

Nature – Lines and Shapes

Often at times, I look and wonder
Is it caused by wind, or thunder?
The twisted shapes of trees, I see
Near the ocean or the sea

Gale force winds would help to shape
Particularly those along the Cape
With the soft earth caused by rain
Help them lean, as though in pain

As the trees grow through the years
Top heavy then, it seems there's fears
Can the roots, so deep in earth
Maintain the tree for all its worth

As drought creeps across the land
The trees in loam and some in sand
Fight the fight to stay upright
Through the day and into night.

Nature's Band

Have you listened to the music of Mother Nature's band
Where the birds and bees gather, to lend a helping hand
As they gather in the pollen, with the buzzing of a song
Then the calling of a night owl, calling deep, low and long?

Hear the ripples of the waters, as they cascade down the fall
And the singing of the magpies, as they warble on the wall
While the mud larks sing a welcome to an early rising sun
The mother deer calls welcome to her playful, wayward son

The frogs upon the mud pool, calling loudly for a mate
While the timid, wily dingo, questions his own fate
Black swans upon the water, honk with morning joy
A puppy on the shoreline, yapping to a little boy

The cattle, in the paddock, let out a mournful call
As the yapping of the kelpie, force them into a ball
The plover, flying over, lets out a startled screech
As it dives downward at a pussy on the beach

A gentle zephyr blowing, causing leaves to sway and dance
And the brolgas of the inland, flap wings and spritely prance
Even pigs let out a chorus, as their dinner time comes round
Old emu puts on a showing, as he thumps upon the ground

We have listened to the music produced by nature every day
And the beauty of the orchestra, it is free, don't have to pay
So take the time and listen to the sights and sounds around
And be proud to be an Aussie, with a real Australian band.

Nature's Call

We see the wrath of nature,
Across this land called Earth
With fires, floods and famine
And pandemic to the fore

This land of trees and forests
Of creeks and river streams
Mountain range and valleys
And pasture lands so green

To see the giant gorillas
Amongst the forest greens
The hippos in lakes and rivers
Koalas in gum trees

This land displays its beauty
It's there for all to see
Splendour and majestic
In a land so proud to be

Then came the hungry miners
Their fortune for, to make
Rejects this land of beauty
For what lay underneath

With fossil fuel around us
The land was soon lay bare
To feed the hungry engines
And make the world go round

World temperatures increasing
Along at rapid pace
While Mother Nature's working
Could not keep up the pace

In measures so demanding
She brought on drought and fires
Then came the flooding rains
For clean and healthy air

So now a battle fury
To restore peace to our earth
And when the battles over
We pray that nature wins.

Nature – Seasons and Weathers

Seasons come but once each year
Bringing forth its weather, clear
Summer, Winter, Autumn, Spring
Let us hear the weather ring

Summer brings the heat and sun
For most it brings the thought of fun
But as the months drag slowly by
We see a change up in the sky

Autumn then is soon to come
The nights are cool, a muffled sun
The days are bright, but cooling down
Lights come on early over town

Winter now, a difficult season
Ice and snow, within reason
Trees denuded, grasses brown
Heaters burning throughout town

Spring arrives with burst of colours
Preferred by me to all the others
Sun and warmth will soon arrive
Makes me glad, I'm still alive.

Nature's Revenge

The sky is clouding over, the sun has lost its shine
There's a stillness in the air, yet the forecast said its "fine"
Clouds are racing onward, like horses in a race
The wind is blowing strongly to keep up with the pace

The thunder sends a warning, lightning flashes bright
Birds have heard the warning and hurry off in flight
The horses in the paddock, let out a frenzied call
While heavy drops of water soon begin to fall

Rain falls down in torrents, day as dark as night
Water on the roadway, racing as if in fright
Into the local river, awake from months of dry
Taking all before it, let's out a mournful cry

Rain continues onward, no hint of break in sight
River run a banker, locals locked into a fight
Against the rushing waters, invading homes at will
Soon the muddy waters are up to the windowsill

Rescues now are needed, boats and men on hand
It's hard upon the water, to see uncovered land
All night the rain keeps falling, new records now to make
This town of seven thousand, now sitting in a lake

For days the rivers flooded, racing on to sea
The local sit and ponder, and wonder what will be
While nature, in its wisdom, works to clear the air
To restore this earth once more, with tender, loving care.

New Zealand

In the land of "the long white cloud"
Where the Maori natives crowd
Where the kiwi loves to play
And the skies are seldom grey

Where the white capped mountains lay
There the seasoned skiers play
It's a place for all to see
Just the place you want to be

Where the kiwi walks the streets
And the sheep, in numbers, bleat
While the Haka hits the beat
To the sound of stamping feet.

Nice

She is tall, blonde and beautiful
Dressed in a T shirt and skirt
Upon the T shirt's wording
We're words that makes one flirt

I stood and looked and pondered
As the words so neatly said
"Nice, till proven naughty"
We're the words that I had read

My mind now in a turmoil
Not knowing where to look
Till the doctor's receptionist called
"Please come and sign this book"

I left the doctor's surgery
To the chemist next, I'm bound
Put in my prescriptions
And the blonde was there, I found

I didn't find her naughty
But instead, she's very nice
I know her hubby's lucky
To have such a lovely wife.

Night Before

T'was the night before Christmas, and Santa was bound
Bound and tied by some murderous hound
Who wanted the toys of the good girls and boys
Computers and lollies, not just the toys

The night was so dark, no stars to be seen
This is the work of some devilish scheme
Santa was trying so hard to be free
To travel the skies and over the sea

The reindeer had gathered, awaiting the sleigh
Santa's helpers ready to help on the way
But where is Santa, they wanted to know
He's tied up and covered in two feet of snow

Rudolf, the reindeer, to the rescue on show
Red nose flashing, he raked at the snow
A red Santa coat was soon to be seen
They all know now where Santa had been

Soon he's recovered and set on the sleigh
Getting things going without a delay
The joy of children all over the land
Can now have Christmas as they had planned.

Night Before Christmas in Aussie Land

T'was the night before Christmas, there wasn't a
    sound
Not a possum was stirring, no one was around
We'd left on the table some tucker and beer,
Hoping that Santa Claus soon would be here!

We children were snuggled up safe in our beds,
With dreams of Pavlova danced round in our heads
And Mum in her nighty, and Dad in his shorts,
Had just settled down to watch TV sports

When outside the house a mad ruckus arose
Loud squeaking and banging woke us from our doze
We ran to the screen door, peeked cautiously out
Snuck onto the deck, then let out a shout.

Guess what had woken us up from our snooze
But a rusty old ute, pulled by eight mighty 'roos
The cheerful man driving was giggling with glee
And we both knew at once who this plump bloke
    must be

Now, I'm telling the truth, it's all dinki-di
Those eight kangaroos fairly soared through the sky,
Santa leaned out the window to pull at the reins.
And encouraged the 'roos, by calling their names.

'Now, Kylie! Now, Kristy! Now Shazza and Shane
On Kipper! On, Skipper! On, Bazza and Wayne!
Park up on the water tank. Grab a quick drink,
I'll scoot down the gum tree. Be back in a wink.

So up to the tank those kangaroos flew
With the Ute full of toys, and Santa Claus too
He slid down the gum tree and jumped to the
    ground,
Then in through the window he sprang with a bound.

He had bright sunburned cheeks and a milky white
    beard
A jolly old joker was how he appeared.
He wore red stubby shorts and old thongs on his feet
And a hat of deep Crimson as shade from the heat

His eyes - bright as opals - Oh, how they twinkled
And, like a goanna, his skin was quite wrinkled
His shirt was stretched over a round bulging belly
Which shook when he moved, like a plate full of jelly

A fat stack of prezzies he flung from his back
And he looked like a swaggie unfastening his pack
He spoke not a word, but bent down on one knee
To position our goodies beneath the Yule tree

Surfboard and footy-ball shapes for us two
And for Dad, tongs to use on his new barbecue
A mysterious package he left for our Mum
Then he turns and he winked and he held up his
    thumb!

He strolled out on deck and his 'roos came on cue
Flung his sack in the back and prepared to shoot
    through
He bellowed out loud as they swooped past the gate
MERRY CHRISTMAS TO ALL, AND
    GOODONYA MATES!

Nightfall

The night birds call, the shadows fell
In the distance, a lone church bell
A dark blanket thrown over town
As if to keep town noises down

Lights come on, as night is here
Sun moved on to another sphere
Babes in bed as mothers rest
The time of night, its mother's best

A silvery moon sends out its glow
Casting light on the waters flow
Boats seen bobbing on the lake
Fisherman using the last of bait

Life moves on in this rural town
Moonlight weakens, clouds frown down
A land at peace, or so it seems
A land asleep, in a world of dreams

On the distant horizon a crack we see
A flash of light coming from the sea
Another day, soon to be born
As life returns in the early morn.

Ninety Years On

After ninety years of use, the engine going fine
Chassis still working but looking worse with time
Lights need adjusting, they're starting to drop
But she is still working, there's no need to stop

Hard to get started, first thing in the morn
But a shove and a push then everything's norm
Fill up her tank, she's hard then to stop
At the end of her run, she's ready to drop

The exhaust is still working, no need for a test
Don't stand behind her, it's one of the best
The lifeline still working, just give her a choke
This one is a "goer" and that is no joke.

The sunlight is shining, she's out for a break
After having a large porter house steak
No insurance for her, the insurer has said
Any time now we're afraid she'll be dead

But ninety odd years is a long time together
We've been around in all kinds of weather
With the help of the Lord and our local quack
We've still miles to go on our life's track.

Norfolk

Norfolk Island, the jewel in the sea
Delightful, majestic, her sights you must see
The sights of the Island, a joy to behold
There's more to this story, yet to be told

Days of the Bounty, etched into time
Proud are the people, mentioned in rhyme
From Pitcairn they came, in boats, they did roam
To make Norfolk their new tribal home

Then from England, the convicts soon came
Men and women, in rags and in chain
Condemned to life, as hard as it comes
Arrived without welcome, no sign of drums

This Island called home, a burden to bare
A prison was built, for protection and care
Yet out of this horror, beauty is seen
On this Island today, peace is supreme

Days of the past, abounds here today
Locals contented, they have their say
Beauty abounds wherever you look
Proudly displayed like a travel book.

Ode to Age

When I was just a little lad, upon my mother's knee
She told me of many things that lay ahead for me
Preparing me for a life ahead and things that I
    should know
I listened hard as she spoke and let my thoughts
    just flow

T'was off to school when I was five, I had a little
    tear.
I learnt the lessons I was told, but with a touch of
    fear.
The lessons that I absorbed, have stuck with me
    I'm sure
Trying hard to like them all but some were such a
    bore

Leaving school, I went to work to earn my board
    and keep
To put my learnings into facts, it was quite a
    difficult feat
But as my learning extended and I felt more at ease
The working tasks that faced me were really quite
    a breeze

By now I'm nearly twenty and looking for a change
I extended my horizons and widened out my range
I moved into the city, a timid, country boy
To further my expectations and to find a little joy

Soon my working life is over, they throw me on a
	heap
They think that I'll retire and sit all day and sleep
Now I'm the boss of my life, no orders do I take
I'll sail around the oceans, leave worries in my wake

When my sailing is over, the world is still my clam
I'll travel on regardless, or just while ever that I can
I find that we, the oldies, have resources by the ton
Should keep on going, and enjoy life and its fun

Now I'm nearly ninety, my times not over yet
There's many miles of travel in this old joker's set
But when the master's ready I guess I'll pack and go
And those that's left behind, a party they can throw.

Ode to the Plovers

I look through my window and see fighting erupt
It's with the crochet ladies, but that's not corrupt
But the nesting plovers, think they're in the right
And to protect their babies, are ready to fight

The father swoops, while the shocked ladies flee
Huddled under protection, they're waiting to see
The plovers are united, the mother at rest
While the croquet ladies wonder what is best

The plovers are the winners, as the ladies call it done
Pack their goods and chattel, and try other fun
The plovers swoop and chortle, and return to nest
The father returns and squats down to rest

For days it is quiet, no sight of the ladies
Yet joy for the plovers, they have four babies
They're up and about, with running and pecking
All round the green and onto the decking

Then sadly, I state, the four babies died
For the parents I'm sad, but bravely they tried
A cold crochet court is hardly the place
To rear young babies to further their race.

Off to Work

As I was on my way to work
Behind me was a teen age jerk
A P plate was upon his van
I guess he thought he was a man

A long blast upon his horn
A pity he was even born
Nothing there to show his age
Yet he seems set on roadside rage

Tried so hard to ignore this man
Stopping now was not my plan
Attempted then, he made a pass
But the road had narrowed fast

Ignored him there, just like I should
He acted like a common hood
I left him there, within my wake
It's to my work that I should make.

Oh Deer, Christmas is Near

Oh deer, Christmas is near
Santa and reindeer are coming, I fear
Children are laughing and looking around
At Christmas shopping all over town

Shop keepers grinning and rubbing their hands
Preparing their shops, the best in the land
Windows displayed with Santa Claus toys
Tempting parents to buy for girls and for boys

The cash register ringing its usual song
Don't keep them waiting, it won't be too long
For Santa has left his home in Lapland
Be on the lookout for when his sleigh lands

Lights on the trees, the big and the small
Gifts are attached, just watch they don't fall
Waiting for children, the good ones, I'm sure
With biscuits and lollies, there's sure to be more

Joy and delight, for Christmas is near
The voices of children, delightful to hear
Singing the tunes of Christmas time songs
In shorts and singlets and a pair of old thongs

Will Santa be having his usual team?
Pulling his sleigh, with Rudolph, I mean
With Dasher and Dancer and all of the boys
I hope that his sleigh is covered with toys.

Old Snake

The slithery snake, slid through the grass
As he's done so, in the past
Searching there for anything
Whether on legs or on the wing

Silently he lays there, just in wait
To see what's there to temps its fate
Soon a victim comes into sight
The snake then takes it in one bite

A field mouse who was full of pride
Soon found he'd nowhere to hide
Old snake was ready then to strike
Then took the mouse without a fight

His tummy now was over full
He's curl up in a bale of wool
To laze away for a day or two
Before he started out anew

The weather now was turning cool
Old man snake was nobody's fool
He'd lay out in the autumn sun
While all around were having fun

Winter brings on cold and snow
Old snake knows where he's to go
Into a hollow log, he's found
And there he'll stay, winter bound.

Old Telegraph Station

It stands alone, way out in the west
The old Telegraph Station, one of the best
For many years it linked south to the north
Morse code back then was really a force

Outside of Alice, like a sentinel, it stands
Loved and adored by its many fans
Its history spans several hundred years
Earned back then with blood, sweat and tears

A pick and a shovel and a crowbar at best
Used by the builders and put to the test
From up in the north a target was set
Erecting a line from Darwin to Alice was met

The buildings erected in time and in pace
To meet with the schedule, as if in a race
It stands there today, as it was in the past
In years to come, I hope it will last.

Old Woodenhead

He's standing looking straight at me
No movement of his eyes, can I see
Mouth so full, he cannot speak
He's been standing there many a week

His neck is scrawny, the skin so roughhouse
From what I see, he must be tough
The nose is like a lump of wood
Who could love him, no one could

He has bars surrounding him
I guess they are there to keep him in
The poor old chap, what's his life
No woman wants to be his wife

While he's standing so stately there
No need for him to comb his hair
The wind may blow, he'll not worry
He's going nowhere, in a hurry

Ugly though is an ugly word
And judging by the words I've heard
Ugly like beauty, if I can be bolder
Is in the eye of the beholder

He looks at home among the trees
Ignorant to many people's pleas
I'll give you a name, I'll call you Jock
You look like "a chip off the old block".

Olympics

Across the skies, they're Paris bound
Aussie athletes that we have found
We've runners, swimmers and divers too
All from the land of the kangaroo

The green and gold, they wear with pride
They all belong to the Aussie side
Working hard, just to be the best
For when they're put to the final test

Into the waters, the swimmers dive
Lap after lap they swim with pride
Waters foam, as they cut through
They don't want to be number two

The ring is where the boxers meet
Fight and fight to win their heat
Onward then, to win their gold
With many stories to be told

Runners, in the heat of day
That's the price they have to pay
Many K's they have to go
A medal then, they have to show

Divers, with their boards up high
Take a dive down through the skies
In ones and twos, they work with pride
Heads pop up, a perfect dive

Hundreds more to hit their tracks
Whether in singles or in packs
Put their hearts in work and fun
To put Australia in number one

The Olympic Games, a worldwide show
A hundred nations on the go
Aussies with their medal haul
We welcome home, one and all.

Once Was the Time

Once was the time when this land of ours
Was won by men with horse and ploughs
Tilled the earth and grew the grain
Sent to the cities by road and train

The rain came down; the rivers ran true
Our paddocks green and sky so blue
Fresh air abounds, no fees to pay
Not the way that it is today

Mines today have scarred our land
Smoke stacks belch, as scientists planned
The rivers run, but not pristine
These are a few things I have seen

The forests now are not the same
Gentle rain is now flooding rain
Our earth is sick, volcanos blow
Tsunamis now a constant flow

This earth of ours in fifty years
People live in constant fears
Can this earth sustain the lot?
I shan't worry, I'll be in my plot.

One Day at a Time

Feeling pain in the chest and not doing well
Went to the doctors to see what he'd tell
A pill and some rest and you'll feel just fine
Just remember to live one day at a time

Don't worry what might happen next year
Live all your days without any fear
The days of the past cannot be repeated
If you follow on that, you won't be defeated

Let life flow as you head for tomorrow
There's pleasure and joy, maybe sorrow
Life is just fine if you play it that way
Just wait till tomorrow, to work out that day

Live for today, enjoy what you do
Enjoy the company, to help you through
I've thought it all through, life is devine
So remember to live one day at a time.

Online Dating

Is my hearing still OK?
Is this what I heard them say?
Online dating Computer Pals way
Let me have a little say

Members then, I ask you if
Your face and figure entered with
Newcastle computer muster team
Imagine what the crowd might seem

Phone numbers flying here and there
Photos flying everywhere
Members increase by the score
Others waiting more and more

Perhaps if my hearing aids go in
And I question once again
Is it right, the thing I thought?
Or is it just another rort?

Only the Lonely

Another day has started
While the loneliness goes on
With ten hours of daylight
I count them right along

With the joints and bones rebelling
And the actions not so fast
Where's the surge of energy
That I had then, in the past

I sit and think and wonder
As the days go quickly past
Of the days when I was younger
And time didn't move so fast

Though the years are going quickly
My mind is still quite sharp
And I consider, rightly
It's not time to play a harp

If you would consider for a moment
That I have feelings too
And need your love and comfort
To spend more time with you.

Open

Open all hours states the sign on the door
Open all hours, that means twenty four
Whenever you're passing, by night or by day
We're open for business, what more can I say

We're here just to serve you
Be it one or it's two
The choices are many, this I am sure
This you'll find out when you pass through the door

The specials are listed up on the board
You'll see our food stuff nicely stored
There's tin food, biscuits, even some bread
Remember your children, keep them well fed

We've chocolates, crackers and the usual chips
These go well if you us them in dips
Wines and spirits in the next aisle to see
All you'll need for a long weekend spree

Let's not forget the perishable stuff
Do all your checks, don't leave in a rush
Got you fruit and veggies? But this I explore
When you go out, please leave open the door.

Our Attic

It's an old house that we live in
Built one hundred years ago
It's one of many in our street
One long, unbroken row

Some of our rooms are spacious
While others are quite small
There's a cellar down below the ground
And a staircase in the hall

Upstairs, above the landing
There is a very small trapdoor
That leads into the attic
Used as a lumber store

Someday I'll pluck up courage
And explore that gloomy space
That lies beneath the roof tiles
That dark, mysterious place

Who knows what secret treasures
In dusty corners stand
Or faded old love letters
Tied with a purple band?

Our Board Secretary

Many's the times I have a thought
For information I have sought
Who do I turn to, wonders I
Ring Susan, with a twinkle in my eye

The board secretary, who's never bored
But of the information she has stored
She answers quickly, I worry not
The answer seems to hit the spot.

A pleasant lass, of this I know
I'll miss her when she has to go
Her time is up, three years they say
A board secretary we do not pay.

AUSOM has this awesome one
With Susan we've had lots of fun
Retire again but do not roam
For ASCCA is your daytime home.

Our Christmas

I had moved to the city, married and settled down but still missing the country life, so had decided spending the Christmas period with my brother, a poet, and his family, still living in the country.

We still had several weeks before we were to leave so had not done a lot towards our Christmas break. My wife was busy buying for all the family which included gifts for my brother and his family. she loves shopping and willingly accepted this task.

The festive season had started at work with parties going on each afternoon for the week. It seemed that all was at peace with the world and hoped this would continue through to the New Year.

This was not to be for just days before departure I received a letter from him stating the following:-

Our Christmas

It's Christmas week, I'm working alone
Stopped my work to answer the phone
A fire has ravaged my in-laws home
She's coming to live in my home of stone

So close to Christmas, what can I do
Said she was welcome, her pussy cat too
Can't let it stop Santa and crew
He's on his way, let's help him through

So for Santa, Christmas is near
Santa and reindeer are coming, I hear
Children are laughing and looking around
At Christmas shopping all over town

Shopkeepers grinning and rubbing their hands
Preparing their shops, the best in the land
Windows displayed with Santa Claus toys
Tempting parents to buy, for girls and for boys

The cash register ringing its usual song
Don't keep them waiting, it won't be too long
For Santa has left his home in Lapland
Be on the lookout for when his sleigh lands

Lights on the trees, the big and the small
Gifts are attached, just watch they don't fall
Waiting for children, the good ones I'm sure
With biscuits and lollies, there's sure to be more

Joy and delight, for Christmas in near
The voices of children, delightful to hear
Singing the tunes of Christmas time songs
In shorts and singlets and a pair of old thongs

Will Santa be having his usual team?
Pulling the sleigh, with Rudolph I mean
With Dasher and Dancer and all of the boys
I hope that his sleigh is covered with toys

When his day is over, I'll start with my own
Looking to find Ma a nice brand new home
Until that day happens, no peace here for me
Hope Santa can fit a new home on our tree

I hope that you, brother, will forgive of me
For Ma in law has nothing, you see
From our family to yours, this I do say
Merry Christmas to all and have a good day.

We were all a little put out but these things happen in life and we did not want to see his Ma in law without a place over Christmas. We, on the other hand, decided that we would spend our Christmas day at the zoo.

This turned out to be a great decision for the day turned out to be a fine, slightly overcast day and every exhibit we visited at the zoo we had eye contact, at least, with an animal of some type.

Just weeks into the New Year I had further correspondence from my brother to advise that his mother in law was established in a new house.

Our Editor

The editor of our Newsletter, a woman so refined
I'd tell you more about her, if I only had the time
Writes a smashing paper, but not always out on time
The stories that she tells of, have rhythm and of
    rhyme

It's all about the "oldies" and stories that they like
If you do not like them, you can just get on your bike
There are jokes and poems and stories too
If you're feeling lonely, well, she'll tell you what to do

And then like Superman, she'll tell you how to Zoom
If you cannot follow, then the brain is set for doom
But read the funny stories, the ones you won't believe
Then sit and have a coffee, and let yourself relieve

This editor of our paper is not one that you should
    cross
For in a shooting moment, she'll tell you who is boss
But this tried and tested lady, yes a lady I did say
Will get the best of everyone, and by hell, she'll
    make you pay.

Our Golden Crop

Paralympics are over, I cry with delight
Each Olympian has put up a great fight
For self and for country, a bag full of gold
Their Nation will take them back into the fold

Names of the winners flashed onto the screens
Following years of hard work and big dreams
Our Aussie group, eighty medals they took
It's like writing a story in a fairytale book

On day one the weather was cool
Swimmers were heading out into the pool
The green and gold of the Aussie fold
Brought home eight medals, all in gold

For two weeks long, the competitors roared
No sight or sound of anyone bored
Spectators here, none to be seen
They were locked up, for covid19

Many an athlete, deserved of fame
Too many to announce each one by name
Needless to say, they all deserve gold
The good, the bed, the timid, the bold

Each and every, they put forward their best
No one could blame them for anything less
Proud was I, that I saw these games
God bless and keep you, you all deserve fame.

Our Lake Macquarie

On the shores of our lake there's much to see
Upon the waters, that come in from the sea
Relax by the shore, or a barbecue there
Lay back and take in the fresh salty air

Always you see boats there afloat
Keeping mariners tending their boat
Even the children, awake and aware
Making the most of what's offered there

As the sun moves around a pattern is shown
Casting the shadows of trees that have grown
Questions are asked about the size of the lake
United we stand and the pride we do take

A great day can be had on the lake, or the shore
Ready and willing, always looking for more
It always remains the pride of our day
Enjoy it, my friends, it's here to stay.

Our Matildas

Out on the field our Matildas go
United they stand and on show

Ready to take the Pommies on
Make it quick, don't take long

Aussie fans are behind your team
To help you all fulfil your dream

In for a penny, in for a pound
Let our girls make good ground

Deny the Poms their winning chance
All in Aussie, we give you thanks
So in you go, and we wish you well.

Our Nurses

In times of extreme, our nurses are there
To help and to aid and treat you with care
Be it labour or ops and all in between
You're in good hands with these lovely Queens

Then came pandemic, and the terrible years
Where each one of us have to live with our fears
Two jabs in the arms, to keep it at bay
With help from the Lord, this we must pray

The I C U and the hospital wards
Keep many of you "flat to the boards"
Isolation it is, for those with the curse
No family allowed, this is the worst

Nurses take over the family ties
Holding the hands of those who have died
With no one to comfort, no one allowed in
Dear Lord, I'm thinking this is a sin

Battle on you must, what a beautiful lot
Without you, I know, we'd all be so lost
With hope and wishes, from millions of us
To control this pandemic, is really a must.

Carry on nurses, you do yourselves proud
We stand and salute you, our heads in a bough
The fate of our nation lay upon your shoulders
And a monument made from Australia's fine
    boulders.

Our Sister

He's taken you, our sister Gwen
You've been with us, from way back when
Just on ninety years, it's been
From toddler to old age, we've seen

Times were tough, when we were young
But as kids it was lots of fun
Growing up, not knowing what
But we handled it, we took the lot

School seemed just to fill in time
In fun and games you'd always shine
Kindness to your peers, we saw
Not standing back behind the door

School's behind you, work you must
Until you met this man you trust
Married him, no looking back
Walked with him down natures track

New Guinea then, was next to be
A soldier's wife, as we could see
Before returning, one time more
To old Aussie's sunny shore

Then fate stepped in and took you man
He was your life, your biggest fan
You settle back, you're now alone
Your dog and you in an empty home

To Queensland now, you decide to go
Up there where you don't see snow
Put down roots and there you stay
Until you reach that final day

Your times been long, you've travelled well
But now it's become a time of farewell
From one and all, we wish to say
Go in peace, and with God, we pray.

Our Travel

I'll tell you a story of places we've been
Of beautiful sights that we have seen
Start off at Sydney, the place I call home
Then off to Italy, and the city of Rome

Barcelona, in Spain, no rain on the plain
Paris, in France, the place on the Seine
Viewed Northern Lights, oh what a sight
In the Serengeti we had a great fright

London, the place all people must do
Then to Glasgow for the military tattoo
Off to Brussels to see their "little pis"
Iraq and Iran, we gave them a miss

Sailed through the "med" and into the Red
Visited Dubai, what more could be said
A magical city, afloat on the sand
Then into Oman, while close at hand

The U S we visited thirty-three States
Hawaii, Alaska the ones with the rates
Vancouver, a city to rival our own
Flags and buntings all over town

Moscow we stayed, but for only one night
Great Wall of China, we climbed with delight
Pyramids in Egypt and sailed down the Nile
Walked the whole of "The Golden Mile"

There's not much left, on Earth to be seen
We're happy and pleases of where we've been
But I've been thinking, that very soon
I'm buying Dianne a one-way ticket to the moon.

Our Truck

It's been with us for many years
But now our eyes are full of tears
It's been the work horse on our plot
Now suddenly it's gone to rot

For years it's done the heavy load
Always on the gravel road
Taking hay to stock out west
Or used to rid the farmers pests

Motors gone, it's done it's time
Used to work through wet or fine
Tyres too, the worse for wear
Done the miles but now who cares

Time to rest, my worthy friend
No more turns around the bend
One more big blast upon your horn
No work for you on the new morn.

Outback

Out back, were the devils dwell
Water comes from an artesian well
Temperatures peak at a hundred plus
Roads and pastures made of dust

Camels move at a leisure pace
Salt bush grows around the place
Kangaroos hop on tender feet
Little survive in this excessive heat

Out back the country is dry and raw
Things don't grow in a land so poor
Animals scarce for want of water
Things no better across the border

A million years an ocean lay
On this land of sand and clay
But today it's just a wasted land
Is this the way the earth was planned.

'Ow 'Ya Goin', Mate?

You ask me how I'm going.
Aches and pains and breath a-blowing
Knees and legs in constant pain
Had to buy a walking cane

Seems I've lost my appetite
Body not a pretty sight
Back goes out more than me
Trouble making a cup of tea

Sex the number t'ween five and seven
Often think what it's like in heaven
Sit back and wait, for we can't tell
Always a chance of making hell

Upon my head, don't use bay rum
It's as bald as a baby's bum
In my mouth, my teeth are false
Don't even try to do a waltz

Hearing aid within one ear
Makes it easier for me to hear
Shave I have every other day
Don't have anything to say

I have me, a walking frame
Easier when my legs do pain
A bottle too, no, not a red
One that goes beneath the bed

I'm still alive, this I can say
My taxes, I still have to pay
In bed at night I lay so still
After taking a sleeping pill

I'm still in touch with the Lord, I think
But after all, I'm in the pink
No family worries, got no kids
But wouldn't be dead for quids.

Painted Clouds

I sit and watch the clouds rush by
Painting pictures upon the sky
A rider sits on a painted horse
Sets out upon a well-worn course

He's headed off, into outer space
A mermaid now will take his place
Until the wind, in hurried pace
Has left her now without a face

The dancers then come on the scene
Swirling around, as if in a dream
Scattering shadows to and fro
Before they, too, have to go

Dark clouds now upon the scene
Where the gentle white had been
Making things look very plain
That soon we're in for heavy rain

The thunder roars, the lightning flash
Upon the land, the waters crash
The eddies form, the gutters flow
How long it lasts, we do not know

The clouds have cried, their waters done
Creek and river again will run
The grass is green, the trees in bloom
The sun's return, will be with us soon.

Paper Chase

The humble roll of toilet paper, this I have been told
On the supermarket store, more precious than gold
Since the news of viruses, is flooding round the track
I'd better go and see a store and get myself a pack

The store is there, for all to see but not a roll in sight
Two ladies there, with trolling high but they were in a fight
I don't know what the fights about, until I see a pack
It's filled with toilet rolls you see, but none upon the rack

This little roll of toilet paper, it's kept in every home
Even take some with you, if you decide to roam
But what's the heck of hoarding it, it won't go out of fashion
It's just to keep it there, if that's your bleeding passion

If things get bad and rolls have gone, I know what I will do
I'll cut the Daily News in shreds and hang 'em in the loo
Things can't get worse, or people can't get dumber
The moral of the story is, it's really just a bummer.

Paralympics

I sat and watch in wonder and awe
The things on Tele I've witnessed and saw
It's the Paralympics that I'm talking about
Such actions and courage, I get up and shout

One legged riders, I've not seen that before
I couldn't cope, even if I had two more
The girls in their bikes, no legs there in sight
But on the track, they roar and they fight

The gold is their aim, the best of the lot
Each one of them give the best that they've got
Be they blind, or they're deaf, outcome is the same
They played with the best, in these sporting games

Came in as strangers, they'll leave here as mates
No place in their hearts, to fit in "the hates"
The sake of their country, the thing they hold high
For the pride of their country, they get in and try

The joy to the watchers, a thing to behold
With each athlete taken into the fold
When this is over, you'll return to your home
With pride and distinction and actions you've shown.

Passing Ships

As the sun goes down on a brilliant day
The clouds come out to make their play
A liner heads out for the open sea
With passengers there to watch with glee

Purple clouds come on the scene
Taking the place where the sun had been
Ships lights are on; it's full speed ahead
With passengers contented and well fed

The Coral Sea, so deep and smooth
Makes it ideal for a winter's cruise
On night's approach, a breeze sets in
Conditions right for those within

With night full on, it's time to play
Let old Satan have his way
Life's so short, let's make it pay
For tomorrow is yet another day.

Pass the Door

If in China you should be
Wander around so live and free
But before that you should stay
Learn your English, China's way

Upon the door of my room there
A sign to tell me, and with care
What to do with my big hands
But I wonder if, and where it lands

Confused, I need Confucius here
He may make the message clear
Until that time I live in fear
Afraid of things that I might hear

Done my time in China town
Bought myself a brand-new gown
Back to Aussie with my pile
To learn English, Aussie style.

Penguins

They stood amongst the snowdrifts
With their backs into the storm
This hardy group of penguins
Huddled up to keep them warm

Then when the storm had finished
And the sun had won the fight
There stood the birds in clusters
In their coats of black and white

Off back into the waters
They scurried very fast
To carry on their fishing
As they had, as in the past

For many miles they travelled
As they hunt for fish galore
And battle many hazards
Before they reach the shore

Life is a battle for the penguin
For there's dangers by the score
But this dapper little seabird
Keep coming back for more.

Planet Earth

God created our planet earth
Created it with all His worth
Where green trees grow and rivers flow
And the gentle breezes blow

But upon this, our promised land
Man was put with work at hand
As can be seen from decades past
Our pristine land just wouldn't last

Man with greed upon their minds
Dug the ground, created mines
Cleared the forests, cut the trees
Fouling up the gentle breeze

Nature then, must take a stand
Sends in plagues upon our land
Floods and famine, we must bear
With pollution to our clean air

Wars and troubles hit our land
Guns and rifles, hand to hand
Until an atomic bomb was sent
With this world, is there no repent?

Still our lessons are not learnt
And our forest brown and burnt
A pandemic now converged on us
Time to act, of this we must.

Platypuses

This world is made of many strange things
Birds that can't fly, although they have wings
A tail on a monkey, but none on an ape
These type of things are what make me gape

But the strangest of all is our platypus
You'll find him waddling out in the bush
Or into the water, is where he's at home
Water reeds and grasses is where he will roam

To look at the build of this little male
Long beak at the front and a broad tail
Feet like a duck, webbed and short legged
For swiftness of swimming, he can't be pegged

A burrow he makes 'neath roots of a tree
All underwater so no one can see
A spur on his legs, poisonous I'm told
Male fighting male, a sight to behold

If you've never seen one in his habitat
It's only because he a cautious young chap
He lives in a stream, where it's dark and it's green
That is the reason why he's seldom seen.

Please be Seated

I said to the tree, "be seated, Sir"
And there he is, seated there
He's been seated there for many years
No one to share his seat, he fears

Through thick and thin, he's carried on
He watches now, right over yon
His seat has become one with him
They were apart when he was slim

They're settled in, a pair for life
Just like a man who takes a wife
No law on land could split them now
Not even if they knew how.

Plover's Return

We have two plovers on our back lawn
I saw them there today at dawn
She's on her nest upon the ground
Some diving now, it will be bound

They had a nest twelve months ago
Four chicks from there they had to show
Fate took hand, the chicks all died
At least they knew that they had tried

So back again, once more to try
So careful as the folk pass by
Ten days to go to hatch her eggs
Peace and quiet, is what she begs

It's in the open, in heat or rain
When all is said, she has a bird brain
I'll keep a watch, see how she copes
They both are clearly full of hopes.

Poems

We've seen the works of Paterson, Wordsworth and even Keats
And read the many stories of their lives and of their feats
Of the many characters they describe, in every poem
Then I get the feeling that, I, too, would like to roam

To be able to put pen to paper, a dream I hold so dear
But my writing capabilities are so lacking, I do fear
If I could confine my dreams to paper, many stories I could tell
But when I wake of mornings, my dreams have gone to hell

I struggle then to make words talk, like famous poets do
Another hundred years I need, for me to make it too
I know I have the words down deep, there's many there, I know
I need to bring the blighters up, and let my talent show

But in the humble way I write, I've stories to be told
I'll write them in the best I can, they not for being sold
Yet in my life I've travelled, and many sights I've seen
I'd like to tell you of these tales, of this I'm very keen

My spirits rather lacking, my pen is running dry
I'll wake up in the morning, and have another try
To tell my travel stories, and try to make them rhyme
I'll sit and think and ponder, and try again next time.

Well, they never found a trace of oil and off they went post haste
I couldn't see a hole so deep just go to flamin' waste
So I moved the dunny over it, real smart move I thought
I'd never have to dig again, and never be caught short

The day I moved the dunny, it looked a proper sight
I didn't dream that poor old Grandad would pass away that night
Now I reckon what has happened, poor Grandad didn't know
The dunny was relocated, when that night he had to go

And you'll probably be wondering how Grandad did his dash?
Well, he used to hold his breath …

Until he heard the splash.

Poor Old Grandad

Poor old Grandad's passed away, was cut off in his prime
He never had a day off crook, he's gone before his time
We found him in the dunny, collapsed there on the seat
A startled look upon his face, his trousers round his feet

The doctor said his heart was good, as fair as any trout
The Constable had to have his say, foul play was not ruled out
There were theories at the inquest of a snake bite with no trace
Of red backs quietly creeping round, and death from outer space

No one had a clue at all, the judge was in some doubt
When dad was called to have his say as to how it came about
Reckon I can clear it up, said dad with trembling breath
You see it's quite a story, but it could explain his death

This 'ere exploration mob' had been looking at our soil
And reckoned that our farm was just the place to look for oil
So they came and put a bore down and said they'd make some trials
They drilled a hole as deep as hell, they said about three miles

Portland Bay

The wind howled, the waves roared
Frightening sailors still on board
The Portland Bay, with power lost
Like a cork at sea, was tossed

Rescue then by aircraft crew
But no use for fierce winds blew
The crew and boat, at nature's mercy
Bobbed about like a headless turkey

Tugboats then with cables, three
Tried to tow the ship to sea
But the ship, laden with cargo
Against the tide, it would not go

Four long days it fought the onslaught
With many lessons to be taught
A break in weather on that day
Allowed the movement of Portland Bay

Into the harbour on a calmer day
Work began on Portland Bay
Released back into calmer ocean
With a gentle rolling motion.

Possum

I was fast asleep in the middle of night
When I awoke in a terrible fright
There were noises above and noises below
I got up, with the bed light aglow.

The noise of a possum, I'm sure it was he
I made a noise, and I saw him flee
A trap I then set, with banana inside
To catch that possum and tan his hide

Early next morning I heard a great din
Up and out, with me after him
Caught in the trap, he had nowhere to flee
It was just him, the possum, and me

Into my van, the possum and me
Drove for an hour, to find a nice tree
Released to door and with banana he fled
Returned to my home and back to my bed.

Problems We Have

My computer isn't working
It won't even talk to me
I'll have to get on to Telstra
To see what it could be

Well Telstra couldn't fix it
But they told me what to do
Told me to contact NBN
But don't put on a blue

NBN came out to see
And said its only dirt and rust
Then said give Telstra another call
They're the ones to trust

And back and forth the story goes
While I'm getting nowhere fast
I think I'll try the ACCC
Like I have done in the past

You little beaut, you'd heard me cry
Telstra and NBN had a little chat
Fixed my problem up so fast
And that's the end of that?

Progress

From long, long ago, I'll tell you a tale
Of the way that we delivered our mail
It came overnight, in bags locked tight
And opened each morning on site

The postie, each morning, upon his red bike
Delivered his letters to post boxes in sight
His whistle he blew, to tell you he's been
Bringing letters and packets so clean

Our telephone calls, a delight for us all
When you rang, a person answered your call
An instance response, from doctors, or such
An answer without any rush

Now progress has blossomed, a sigh of relief
A letter can now take many weeks
The telephone call, we've all heard the clue
Press button one, or press button two

Leave your name and number, we'll call you
My friend, it may be a day, ever two
But progress it is, just ask the snail mail
This progress, I find, makes me quite pale.

Promises, Promises

Vote for us, we'll give you the earth
I listen to this with a great deal of mirth
Never known an honest one yet
I'll take them on with a smirk and a bet

Before they're elected, you're a good guy
After elected, well they don't even try
I'm a sync, I know, I've seen it before
Now if you ask, they'll show you the door

They are there for three years, some even more
But with politics, you know, nothing's for sure
Vote with the party, do as you're told
Don't vote as just one, that's being bold

We live by the way of the party in charge
Some take things easy while others barge
In three years' time, one things for sure
It will start over, they'll be begging for more.

Pussy

There's a lady I know, with a cute little pussy
Only thing wrong, she's a little bit pushy
When Charlie arrives, a dashing young beau
She has her pussy, right there on show

I'm jealous of Charlie, but it must not show
When Charlie arrives his coat is aglow
He does not stay long, he's off in a flash
Home to his mother, for his bowl of mash

That cute little pussy, kept most in the dark
But when released, it's off like a lark
A pat and it's happy, and ready for more
Waits for the opening of the front door

It knows when it's hungry and wants to be fed
Then likes to curl up on a nice feather bed
With all the excitement it's had in the day
All we need know, whose going to play.

Rabbit Trappers

There were rabbits by the thousands
In the towns and country scenes
Two tried and tested trappers
Though yet to reach their teens

Set off with traps and setter
And their terrier at their heels
Found and set their trappings
At the burrows in the fields

In a dark and winters morning
With the sun about to rise
Retraced their plant of settings
Then it's homewards with their prize

Then skin and gut their catches
And peg the skins to dry
Prepare the meat for cooking
For tonight it's rabbit pie

The skins are sent to market
A pound a pound is tendered
A worldly price to us
Money in our pocket, we go home contented.

Recall of the Thirties

I recall the time, way back in the past
When times were tough and didn't move fast
We'd go to town in horse and dray
Do a week's shopping, spend most of the day

Work was so hard, no mechanical savvy
From daylight to dark, they worked like a navvy
No joys like today of phones or T.V.
I guess that's the way it had to be

Cows were milked, twice a day, by hand
By horse and plough, they would dig up the land
Water provided by dams or above
All this done with a labour of love

The years moved on, improvements were made
Electricity provided, for those that had paid
Bread was delivered by horse and cart
Milk in glass bottles – that was the start

Ice boxes were used, to keep the food cool
Swimming in rivers, no one had a pool
Daily at school, you didn't choose
All kids went to school, no one wore shoes

The Second World War changed our world for the better
It would cost two pence, if you posted a letter
Telephones connected, for those who could pay
Our lives now improving, just day by day

The war brought relief, work now for all
Machinery abounds, cars now is the call
Clothes, though rationed, were there to be had
Causalities of war, we heard, was so sad

Life has improved, sliced bread now on the go
Dressed like a star, it's all there on show
Radios and phones are now to be had
I'd say about now, well our life's not so bad.

Recycled

I wandered down to town today
And did some shopping on the way
With fruit and veg and sweets galore
I wondered was there anything more?

So down the aisles I slowly stepped
To where the major goods are kept
And check to see they're Aussie made
The only ones to make the grade

My shopping now is almost through
Bought some stuff to make a stew
Then another aisle I'm yet to see
Before I go to pay my fee

As I head towards the door
A thing I hadn't seen before
Upon the toilet roll I gazed
What I read made me amazed

The toilet roll, I'll have you know
Is not as white as driven snow
The toilet roll that you do buy
From recycled paper, I do spy

They made it smell so nice and sweet
No smell at all like dirty feet
So when you sit upon the loo
There's paperwork for you to do.

Red v Blue

We've heard the story, fake and true
Between America's red and blue
Democrats and Republicans head-to-head
Wants it decided before our bed

Trump with stories wild and fake
Biden for President, he wants to make
Fans of both, with guns and noise
Even hard to tell who's girls or boys

We've won the election, the master told
But the other side, our votes they stole
We want a recount, we'll stop the count
The Electoral officers said no recount

Fights go on between the fans
Reds who want the counting banned
Blues request all votes to count
Electoral counters, on seats they mount

Trump can see his position flagging
Even with his boastful bragging
Now he calls for High Court backing
But for proof, there's something lacking

It seems that though results are final
Court case talk is on the spiral
We'll just have to watch and wait
To learn of America's ultimate fate.

Reflections

I sit today, so deep in though
This life through which I have fought
My mind goes back to yesteryears
When we had the depression fears

No work, no money, just the dole
Had to do as we were told
Hobos by the dozens, roams
Swags upon their backs, their homes

Followed then by World War Two
Five years of war we struggled through
Work and jobs for one and all
Until we heard the war cry call

Korean War called for our men
Many lives were lost then
Followed on, the Vietnam war
We battled on as we have before

Twenty-twenty brought on more strife
Floods, and fire disrupt our life
Then the world was hit by flu
Governments don't know what to do

In isolated silence, I must sit
The brain and mind is still fit
Until the "all clear" is given us
Sit here and wait, is what I must.

Return to the E.R.

I'm back in E R, yet again
With my tummy aches and pain
My nurse then does an E.C.G.
To see what they'll do with me

My temp she takes and B.P. too
Checks for any signs of flu
Covid questions have been asked
I've had the jabs in months past

The stethoscope beneath my vest
Checking lungs are working best
A needle then pushed into my arm
Am assured it will do no harm

An hour then, I lay and wait
I think they're working out my fate
Then a Doc comes on the scene
I wonder now, where has she been

Time moves on, I've had a snooze
A doctor then asks if I use booze
A negative I pass by
I see a tear within his eye

My time is up, I'm going home
No bad response, I'm free to roam
A parting quip, don't come again
Unless you're ill and racked with pain.

Ring Me Back, Will Ya

I rang a friend the other day
To speak of many things
I rang him in the afternoon
But the phone, it just rings

Then after thirty seconds
A recorded voice they play
Just ring me back, will ya?
So, no more could I say

I asked a friend to try him
She tried it eight or nine
But across the vacant line
Came the same result as mine

So across the vacant phone line
The ones you have to pay
Comes the same old chorus
Just ring me back, will ya?

R is for Rooster

R is for rooster, who crows in the morn
Crows for he's asking for his morning corn
Waking up neighbours and family alike
Flying around like a lop-sided kite

He'd better be careful as Christmas is near
One wrong move and it cooker, I fear
But after all, he's chickens to rear
So chase up the hens, there's duty to bare

His colour is bright, of the Rhode Island Red
While crossing the road, he thought he was dead
A man on a bike of indeterminable age
Yelled at the rooster, in quite a rage

Rooster escaped with hardly a scratch
The motor bike rider was really no match
With a crow and a cackle, was full speed ahead
Reaching his roost, he laid down his head.

Content with his lot, he settled right down
Chasing the hen, a deep shade of brown
Cornered at last, she lay on her feet
And the poor old rooster admitted defeat.

Road to Ruin

I was on my way to work one day
Went along my usual way
There upon the road I found
A hole, so deep, within the ground

Couldn't stop, so in I went
Wife and I and little car, were sent
Into this hole that swallowed us
It really caused a lot of fuss

There's a piece of road within the hole
My wife called out to me so bold
I lost control, I'm sad to say
I guess for this I'll have to pay

All's not over yet, I think
I'm really in an awful stink
To find a way from in this hole
Will take some time, or this I'm told.

Rudolf, in Retirement

Santa Clause is coming again
Though his face is covered in pain
For Rudolph is staying at home
No more he is able to roam

The light has gone out of his nose
No light now wherever he goes
He's put out to pasture, I fear
With a herd of young female deer

While Santa is travelling all over
Rudolf is left home, in clover
To replenish the stock of red noses
And fill in the spot that it poses

A Santa more slimmer and nimbly
Is more able to fit down the chimney
But his red and white suit is covered in soot
As is his arms and his legs and his foot

But Rudolf, at home, not a shirker
From the sight of the doe's, he's a worker
And when Santa gets home from his travel
There'll be kids and more kids in a rabble.

Santa's Journey

Santa from his world of snow
In the Lapland forest's glow
With his reindeers, fleet of foot
Preparing for his worldly trip

Santa with his sleigh packed high
Dashing through the evening sky
Seeking out the girls and boys
To fill their socks with many toys

Girls and boys from many lands
Know of Santa and his plans
Go to bed with hearts aglow
Waiting for their Christmas show

Morning comes, their eyes so bright
Looking at the many sights
Running here and running there
Showing off a new found bear

Santa then, his race now done
Happy with the children's fun
Turns his charges, heads for home
One year's time once more he'll roam.

Santa's Lot

From the far off distant land
Where the midnight sun is found
Lives a man we all adore
We welcome with an open door

Santa Claus is who I mean
The idol of all children's dream
He settles in, to pack his sleigh
Before he sets out on his way

Phones and lap tops by the score
Been requested by more and more
On and on the list still comes
Some even wants kettle drums

The packing's done, at nights approach
Wrapped up like a prince's coach
The reindeer waiting in the wings
Ready to start when Santa sings

Ho Ho Ho, the merry song
Ready now to start along
The reindeer leap into their flight
To get there in the dead of night

Chimneys entered through the night
Should see Santa, quite a sight
Covered now from head to foot
With a coating of black soot

Children waking in the morn
Feeling great that they were born
Opening presents, to see and show
And Santa's back in the land of snow.

Santa's New Helper

No more do we see Rudolf and boys
Santa has a new helper for his toys
Prices have risen for reindeer upkeep
He's turned them out to forage and sleep

His incoming helper loves girls and boys
She's just the one to deliver his toys
Flies like a witch, up into the air
Up through the sleet, without a care

No more we hear the jingle of bells
A blast of a horn is all that it tells
Inflation is high, it's up in the sky
Santa's helper can help, at least she'll try

So children, beware and try to be good
Always do the things that you should
Santa and helper, I'm sure will be there
When they arrive, give a big cheer.

School Bells

Still I hear the ringing of the bell we had at school
When the teacher used to ring it, they used it as a tool
For it was used to muster and to advise us of the time
Whether it was raining or if the sun would shine

We had gathered on the asphalt, in unregulated lines
And listened to the master, as we have so many times
It was in the thirties, when times were very grim
The seat upon our trousers were very, very thin

Oft I sit and wonder, of the lads that went to school
Of ones who tried to study, and ones who played the fool
"I can teach, but can you learn" I've heard the teacher say
Some can learn the lessons while some of you will pay

In the story of a lifetime, many lessons have been learned
Then I sit and ponder, thinking how the world had turned
Where were my cobbers and my school mates?
Had they learned and what's their fates?

Those of us who lasted, I guess there's only few
Of the ones I went to school with, the ones I really knew
Would be worn and weathered, probably hair white as snow
Those of us that's lived it, had the best of it, I know.

Shadow

In the shadow of the father
Stands a man, yet to be made
As he struggles on and upward
If his courage doesn't fade

He had many years of schooling
As he searches for a trade
And then the constant battle
To keep up with his grades

He has love and understanding
From his parents and his peers
And the friendship of his colleagues
As he treads on through the years

Yet through his years of learning
One thought keeps burning on
Will he be as good as father
When his learning days are done?

The young man now is married
A wife and baby son
Still often he will wonder
Of the race that he has run

Now that shadow's cast
On the new life he has made
In the shadow of the father
Will often be replayed.

She Broke a Bone

Down the stairs, she has a fall
I went down when I heard her call
A groan and curse, I heard in pain
I've broken a bone in my foot again

To the doctor then she made a call
Told them of her nasty fall
They suggested an emergency run
To Belmont hospital, that won't be fun

Home we are to call GPS
Oh, but oh, what a mess
Two hours on the phone but no reply
I can't get through though I must try

Next day at our doctor's room
Two hours we wait, all in gloom
Just to be told an X-ray to be done
There we go, in mid-morning sun

The X-Ray shows a fine bone crack
Back we go to our local Quack
A moon boot on, with crutch I walk
I'm so frustrated, I can scarcely talk

Home I am, my leg at rest
Resting the way that I do best
On the laptop and on the phone
Catching up while I cannot roam.

Shopping Spree

Went to the shops to buy me some bread
Sat on a seat watching people instead
The sights that I saw were hard to describe
I can't explain all, as much as I tried

Oldies in young clothes, a sight to behold
Youngsters in reveal alls, oh to be bold
Tattoos, I ask, just where do they stop
When they get old, I guess they'll just flop.

To keep up with fashion, some say we must
That's only the shops, that is their lust.
Then along comes a " walker" an old fellow in toe
A mask on his face, covers a beard and a mo

Along comes a mother, two kids in a pram
Caught up with a trolley, it's really a jam
That's how it goes, there all in a rush
To get back to Tele, this is a must

The tums and the bums, what is the score
I won't be looking for them any more
I'll sit in the shadows, eyes closed as in sleep
If I open them more, I'm sure I could weep

My eyes open wide, there's just she and me
It's into the car and quickly we flee
Away from noise and motor car drone
Back to our home, where I'm left alone.

Sir Tom

We've watched you do your famous feat
You've walked for miles on tender feet
The millions of pounds kept rolling in
Because of you its win, win, win

They've knighted you, your just deserts
You've overcome your aches and hurts
With men like you, to show the way
Where Queen and country have their say

One hundred years you've battled through
The wars, the struggles, pandemics too
We've heard from you and what you say
"Tomorrow will be, a good day"

The curtains fall, He's taken you
Into His world that's always blue
The world you left, a better place
Memories of you and full of grace.

Smart Phone

She loves her smart phone more than me
Though I'm the one who pays the fee
She keeps it with her day and night
Opens it up at morning's light

It tells the time and weather too
Even tells her what to do
She heeds it more than she does me
It's like a drug to her, you see

When she goes out she'll check to see
That smart phone is there with thee
It's pride of place, it is her life
She doesn't want to be a wife

When smart phone rings, she answers thus
She's not one to make a fuss
But if by chance a scam calls comes
She'll click it off with both her thumbs

Before she starts her life each day
Sees what the weather man does say
Then she plans her leisure time
If the weather is to be fine

She watches tele every night
Mr smart phone is still in sight
She's watching both, I can see
Oft with the laptop on her knee

Life is hard, the pundits say
She just takes life day by day
With the smart phone, she will say
She'll be ready, come what may.

Smiley

I was walking through the park one day
And found a tree along the way
He had a mouth, but wouldn't talk
But too many eyes, is what I thought

His facial features were very grim
No smile upon the lips for him
There's dribble upon his neck, I see
I should turn around and flee

This wooden face that I look at
With signs that show where birds had sat
Even with so many eyes to see
You cannot see behind the tree

With eyes and arms and twisted nose
I guess there's no one who would propose
So then, I say, my wooden friend
You'll stay and snarl until the end.

Snowy

In the foothills of the Snowy
Where the mountain horsemen live
There was rumour that a wealthy horse had got away
He had joined up with the wild bush horses' herd

Panic rode amongst them,
As they sought a distant plain
For they heard the distant whip cracks
Of the riders from the town

The riders rode behind,
Over rocks and boulders bare
Riding onward, ever onward
Fearing nothing as they rode

There was one among the riders
He was young, without a care
Spurred on his sweating stock horse
Without a backward glance, he made the battle his

Across gullies, creeks and deadwood
He rode at lightning speed
Ignoring hurt and hunger
As he pushed his faithful steed

He had left the other riders
Far behind, in worried mood
But the youngster had the measure of the herd
He had reached the furthest, turned them, headed
    home

At the homestead were the others,
Men and horses tired, wet and weary
Yet they lift their heads to see
The lad from Snowy Mountains, bringing tired
horses home.

Snowy Member

There was panic in the Senate
For there was rumour in the air
That the PM, in his wisdom
Called an election for the Spring

It had caused some consternation
In the House and in the Senate
For the members had no warning
And confusion reigned supreme

The Whip was given orders
That the House was soon to rise
And the loyal and trusted members
Had a battle on their hands

For the promises made in hindsight
Could come and bight them, once again
And some sit in silent wonder
For many may never sit again

Election Day was over and voting had been done
There were many weary members
As they turned heads and headed home
The member for the Snowy, the man who brought
    them home.

Soul of Australia

The soul of Australia runs long and runs deep
Father sun shines while Mother Earth weeps
Sun shining bright over heaven and earth
Mother Earth struggles for there's no sign of mirth

Nature sends floods to help replenish the land
Volcanos erupt, to help ease deeper pain
While man keeps spewing out poisonous fumes
Coal and methane helps dance to their tunes

Protests by the people, in countries and town
Muddies the waters and makes a loud sound
Calls to the converted is all that it reaches
Not to those seeking money and riches

A lesson, not learned by those in the lead
Those with the money do not even heed
The end is in sight if somethings not done
Despite the efforts from winds and the sun

Mother Earth suffers, with holes in her side
Until all is taken, nothing left inside
What a horrible sight, land barren and bare
Sun shining down but mothers not there.

Spring

Morning has broken, the sun shining bright
Melting the frost that was left overnight
The cobwebs are covered in a fairy like mist
While the birds are feeding away from their nest

The hills in the distance, treeless and bare
Awaiting the spring, with its fresh, warming air
To burst into growth, with grasses so green
To cover the harshness, where winter has been

The fruit trees are turning buds into flowers
Awaiting the first of spring's gentle showers
The gardens awake, the browns and the greys
Assisted along by the sun's warming rays

The tulips are showing, their buds can be seen
Among all their leaves, so dark and so green
The daffodils in flower, both yellow and white
Making the gardens so colourful and bright

Now winter is leaving, Spring on the way
We'll see minor changes, day after day
The trees of the orchard preparing to bear
And the plants in the garden, we've tendered with
    care

So off with the winter, so cold and so bleak
On with the Spring, though it sun is still weak
And wait for the warmth of a strong Spring sun
To bathe in the warmth and have lots of fun.

Spring Has Sprung

The wind blew in across the bay
Causing the waves to leap and play
The boats at anchor, duck and dive
As on the water, they do drive

Fishermen with their rod and pole
Fishing in their favourite hole
Children heard in laughter, play
Spring has shown its first new day

Grasses green and flowers peep
From their sleep, so long and deep
Bringing forth their coloured bud
From the earth that's sometimes mud

The wind abates, the sun now shows
Children dressed in springtime clothes
Hop and skip, away they go
Parents watch, with eyes aglow

As the day goes on in wonder
In the distance, one hears thunder
Spring has sprung, the birds are singing
To their nest, they'll soon be winging

Other days are yet to come
Before Spring seasons finally done
Get out, enjoy and thank your maker
It's all done by Mother Nature.

Stairway to Heaven

I'm standing here at the stairway to Heaven
The clock showing that it's half past eleven
Soon, I see, I'll be walking these stairs
You can be sure I won't take them in pairs

The time on the clock is running faster than me
I can't turn it back, of this I can see
The sun is going down in the west
But I'm not ready yet for eternal rest

There're things to do, it runs through my head
I must be dreaming, I must be in bed
That clock is still ticking, the hands rushing past
I must do something, and must do it fast

I think of the times, the good and the bad
Many is the times I felt rather sad
Good are the times that make me feel great
But it all depends on that word called fate

I'll sit back and wait and enjoy all that there is
And let that old clock continue to whiz
A spot in the sun, away from the breeze
For I'm not ready for the cold and the freeze

Stock

There's many types of stock, we find
Horses, cattle, sheep and swine
While grocers have a different stock
Upon their shelves, on the corner block

While on those shelves, a different stock
These, we find, are a stock mock
Beef stock, chicken stock, any another stock
But these go into a cooking pot

With politics, all brass and bold
Smug and smart, and won't be told
Are often in for quite a shock
When they become, the laughing-stock.

Suddenly We're Seniors

My working life is over, they've put me out to be
Today is the first of ever, what now's in store for me
I sit and read the paper, and think of work I've done
While my mind still working, I think I'll take a run

There's confusion all around me, don't know what to do
My mind is still for working, my body, still working to
I'll have to find a hobby, to fill the days ahead
There's more to life than worry, as I head for bed

Now I'm thinking sanely, I hang my head and bow
I'm ready for the future, for I'm a senior now
There's travel on my agenda, places there to see
I'll cruise upon the oceans and see the many seas

When travel days are over there's many things to do
Sit and read a magazine, or make a pot of stew
Write about my travels, or a poem or two will tell
There's many groups and services I can join as well

Now I'm senior settled, I've forget I used to work
I had joined a group of seniors, now I am their clerk
I've been many years a senior, no regrets, you see
I will be a senior, until the Lord has called for me.

Summer

Rain is falling, the sun at rest
Flies and mosquitos, a real pest
Days are hot, nights are warm
Summer comes in its usual form

Body sweating, no will to work
Looking for an easy perk
Rest in the shade, drink at hand
Need someone to set up a fan

Doze in the shade, till I hear a sound
Sure it's a mosquito, hunger bound
Squiggle around, till I see him land
He gets a slap with my big hand

Time marches on, near time for tea
Bangers and mash, an occasional pea
A cuppa tea, no it's too warm
To have an ale is the usual form

Another day in the heat and sun
Not much playing, not much fun
Sit around till summers gone
Then I'll have my winter woollies on.

Sunset

Evening shadows linger, as the sun goes down to rest
Casting colours on the waters, making pictures of the best.
A gentle breeze is blowing a very gentle tune
As the day gets ready for an ever present moon

The lighthouse keeper readies for the coming of the night
As he prepares the beacon with the ever flashing light
For a warning to the shipping of the dangers up ahead
Then he may sleep in slumber in his warm and cozy bed

The lightning flashed a warning in the middle of the night
Sending sheets of rainfall, drenching everything in sight
While the wind, in all its fury, sets the ocean in a dance
But the flicking of the lighthouse, is steady in its stance

With the coming of the morning, not a thing seems out of place
The sun and feather clouding seeming ready for a race
And the flashing of the lighthouse completed yet another day
While the ocean, like a mirror, just contented as it lay.

Surprise, Surprise

I took my lady to the Doc's
She told me what to do
Take her home and keep her warm
For I think she's got the flu

So homeward bound I took her
To her bed two metres wide
Covered her with blankets
It's somewhere she could hide

She moaned and groaned and shivered
And called me several times
He temperature going up again
I'm feeling crook, she whines

A water bottle, I delivered
To try and stop the shake
If you don't do something quickly
You'll be going to my wake

The night came on like thunder
Dark and black as pitch
An eerie light was shining
I think I saw a witch

But in the early morning
A shock was there to see
For in this bed between us
Was another, who looked like me

A baby, bright and cheery
A mother, shocked and scared
The father in a panic
For nothing was prepared

The moral of this story
If you're feeling ill at ease
Go see a gynaecologist
Her help will be a breeze.

Take Me Home

Take me back to the home I once knew
Where waters are clear and wonderfully blue
Snow on the mountains to freshen the air
Grasses so green and plentiful there

The draw of the city with bright lights displayed
Took me away from the place where I played
Into a city where the numbers are vast
Forgetting my home and things of the past

The years have rolled on, decisions I've made
Most have gone well, for others I've paid
My journey through life, a bonus for me
But still I don't feel completely free

I'm aged and wrinkled, my hair has gone white
Eyesight and knees, don't fill with delight
Around the world I've travelled and roam
But, please, I ask, just take me back home.

Tales of Gloucester

In the lea of The Buckets, there lay a town
Gloucester lay peacefully, on its hallowed ground
Its river and mountains, beauty they give
A place for the locals to work and to live

I lived in this town, many decades ago
Through childhood and teens, I had my go
Schooled by teachers, their names I recall
Good times and bad, I've had them all

I recall the war, in this small rural town
Young men went to war, UK they were bound
Rations imposed on clothes and food stuff
Grew our own veggies, but still things were rough

In Cook Street, it was, when the camel man came
He and three camels, each one of them tame
Camels and man, in our yard they stayed
My brother and I, with the camels, we played

Two weeks after leaving, Taree he was bound
Advice from police, this man had been found
He was working around as a German spy
I couldn't believe it, as much as I try

Finishing school, to the Post Office I went
Working there until five years were spent
Then off to the "big smoke", Newcastle to be
Still Gloucester remains the hometown for me.

Talking Toilet Seat

"Put your head in the bowl
You'll hear the ocean" I'm told
Inviting and all, with pix on the wall
Just enough room to answer the call

With the colour they have painted
It's enough that I fainted
But when nature has called
It obvious I shouldn't have stalled

When the ocean had roared
I had not heard a chord
For the noise of the water flushing
I'm leaving, I think I'm blushing.

Tarot Anyone?

When I was young and in my prime
I'd visit tarot readers all the time
She'd tell me of my future life
Even said I'd have a redhead wife

She gets her inspiration there
By swiping cards upon her hair
Telling you what waits for you
In this world, so big and blue

A pretty face is what she's not
Usually though she hits the spot
Telling what you want to know
Always with a smile to show

Patrons come from far and near
To listen and from her to hear
Good news from a departed one
Be it a mum or a departed son

The curtain closes, her day at end
She's off home to her old friend
When the new day comes again
Once again she'll relieve your pain.

Taxi

Into the taxi she jumped, quite nude
Those who saw her, thought rude
The driver, thinking more of his purse
Let out with a blast and a curse

The lady spoke out, as she sat
Just what are you looking at?
Have you not seen a nude woman before?
And just look at the drop of your jaw.

With a stutter and stammer he spoke
Lady I'm sure that this is a joke
I looked at your body, that's fair
But, my dear, where are you hiding my fare.

Tea for Two

Teapot is ready, hot water awaits
Everyone here to hear of their fates
Alice is there, sitting close to the door
Father is being his regular bore

Others arriving, waiting for tea
Rogers is scratching a bite from a flea
The weather is right for tea on the lawn
Watched over, no doubt, by the newly born fawn

Oh, said the maid, I must hurry along
Others were singing a Beetle's song
Returned to the fold, the wayward son
To recoup his money, lost on "the run"

We gather around the table and pot
Offers of cake with tea that is hot
Father, I see, is dozing once more
Others now gather around the back door

Ready we must, for the sky's turning dark
Together we'll walk home, up through the park
Enjoyment was had by one and by all
A new day soon dawning, we've all had a ball.

Ted, the Dog

I went to mind a house and a dog they named Ted
When he is with his mistress, he sleeps upon her bed
Yet when I minded him, some three years before
I taught him that his bed was made up upon the floor

He was good and contented, just curled up at my feet
That was until he thought that I was sound asleep
Then like a little devil, to my bed he made a dash
I grabbed him by the collar, and the noise was like a crash

Let out a yelp, jumped off the bed, landed on all fours
To his bed he hurried, with his head upon his paws
He lay there with one eye open, to see what's going on
Decided he'd better play her game, so to sleep he had gone

Next morning, to my side he came, two paws upon my bed
With pleading eyes and waging tail, "get up and get me fed"
A hurried look towards the door, it's time to take a walk
We walked along, there's other dogs, so he has a doggy talk

Two weeks of my training him, I wonder what he'll do
When "mum" gets home from her travels too
And as she snuggles into her big bed
Will she make room in there for Ted?

Test Patience

We sit and watch the game of cricket
Where the bowler tries to take a wicket
The batsman though, with will of iron
Hits the ball and it's gone flying

Fielders race from all directions
Picks up the ball, giving inspection
The ball returned to the bowler's end
He then sends down a curly bend

I hear a noise, what can that be
She's gone to sleep, I finally see
Her snoring there, quite severe, I hear
It's exciting cricket, the ashes, dear

Her snoring though, it's loud and clear
Has no effect on the batsman's fear
He's hit the ball; it's gone for four
Don't think she'll wake to see more

My eyes are heavy, the scoring slow
The batsman's just had a heavy blow
The score creeps on at snail's pace
Does it matter who wins the race

I'll leave her sleep, she needs the rest
A wise man said cricket was a test
The umpire has just called for drinks
Time for me to sleep, me thinks.

That Hat

In Darwin we board the beautiful Ghan
To Adelaide, we hope, that is our plan
A lady boards, neither skinny nor fat
But look at the size of her over-sized hat.

At Katherine we boarded a boat for a spin
Saw a crock, no shark, not even a fin
That lady was there, you could see where she sat
And up on her head sat that horrible hat.

Back on the train, we're called in to dinner
No one on board is getting any thinner
The one I notice, we're all looking at
As in comes that lady, still wearing that hat.

In Alice we had a meal under the stars
Plenty of tinnies but no sign of bars
Who do you think they sat next to me? That
Same little old lady, covered by hat.

In Coober Pedy we went underground
But sadly to say, no opals were found
Her husband was there, in his hand was a bat
I wonder if it's to be used on that fated hat.

Well folk, I tell you, for good or for bad
And worst of all, I was feeling quite sad
For there stood that lady, upon a fine mat
Said she'd donated to Vinnies, that very hat.

That Night

The night was dark and stormy, the lightening flashing bright
With children huddled in their beds, their eyes are closed so tight
A wind was howling round the house, loose objects on the fly
No sleep for the parents on this night, as hard as they may try

Increasing winds are heard by all, as it comes in from the south
The lights are out, the front door groans, there's panic in the house
A bang is heard upon the roof, the dog lets out a yelp
Too late to leave a storm struck home, now they need some help

The rain came down in torrents, the thunder peals and roars
While the parents, in their terror, block off the rattling doors
Once more a clap of thunder, the house is heard to creak
The parents, now exhausted, lay down in troubled sleep

As morning creeps across the plain, a new day has begun
The rain and thunder of the night, has left and on the run
While left behind, the parents find, much must now be done
To clear away the rubble, then sit and take in the sun.

That's Life

The sun comes up, the sun goes down
Shops still closed all over town
No visitors, callers do I see
Lord only knows what's to happen to me

Food supplies are getting low
Tea and coffee just so so.
Perhaps a delivery, on the run
Closest thing to what I call fun

Floors vacuumed, lunch is done
Oh what fun to sit in the sun!
But carry on, it's what I must
With a duster now, to clear the dust

Now dinner is over, I watch TV
Really nothing there to interest me
Re-read the book I read last week
To recall the ending, I have a peak

I tell you, friend, that life is great
To have your dinner on a plate
To break the monotony of the day
Then listen to what the Politicians say.

The Alice

Alice Springs, is the real living heart
Central Australia, playing its part
North or south, east or west
Right in the middle, it is the best

Met with the indigenous Alice Springs mob
Laughed and played, as they did their job
Shocked at the way they have to live
With stories and legion, they have lots to give

To Daly Waters, just a one-horse town
Arrived in town, with the sun going down
Met there a man, just as large as life
Runs the town with the help of his wife

In Darwin's fair city, more sights are seen
The water in harbour so blue and so clean
Met with transvestites and lesbians galore
A night at the club was just what you adore

Two weeks in this city, life is a great feast
You're leaving here now, heading off east
To visit a mine, and talk with the head male
And to see where miners live, a glorified jail

Then get caught up in a rally, they call it a bash
All drivers are cheerful, there's no need for a clash
There're colours and costumes and cars dressed too
You even made use of their portable loo

Turn to the south, it's the Gold Coast you seek
Looks like you'll stay there, at least for a week
With nippers and strangers, you're having some fun
Just walking and roaming around in the sun

Then heading off south, through cities and towns
On roads made for travel, homewards you're bound
You pass on from Sydney and on down the coast
You're sure you're an Aussie, or that is your boast

The journey is over, many sights you have seen
The good, the bad, the ugly, the mean
You've seen Australia, and now you can be
As warm, and lovely and an Aussie, like me.

The American Race

It's known far and wide, the American race
Two men racing to keep up the pace
One dressed in red, the other in blue
A race to decide, the strong and the true

It's run every four years, be it wet or be dry
They go for the throat, give their best try
They start off quite slowly, planning their moves
As things get warmer, they run in their grooves

The one in the red, an ego miles high
The other won't match him, won't even try
But out in the states he'll give him a run
Then sit back and watch, and wait for the fun

It doesn't take long for the blue to take lead
While the one in the red is a different type breed
He huffs and he puffs and calls Joe a big thief
I'm afraid old red is in for some grief

The line's getting closer, the judge on his stand
Crowd getting restless but cheered by the band
I'll sue you, you know, if I do not win
We'll head for the courts to work out your sin

With his toe over the line, the man in the blue
Receives a nod from the judge, you made it through
While the man in the red, the colour of rage
I feel this man should be locked in a cage

This race is not over, the red man exclaimed
He and his crew go on to explain
The theft of the votes that should have been mine
The judge will review it and you will do time

A shoehorn will be needed to remove the red mano
The White House is his, or this is his plan
While the man in the blue, just Biden his time
For the Stars and the Stripes to tell that it's fine.

The Animal Tale

The kookaburra laughed in the early morn
Wombat looked so darn forlorn
Kangaroo and wallaby too
Came out to see what they could do

The red fox darted in and out
To see what the noise was all about
The crocodile smiled with a Leary grin
He knew the mob was onto him

He's into the pool and under water
Knew that they'd give him no quarter
He'd lay there till it was dark
Then come out and make his mark

The koala in his tree top home
Knew there's no need for him to roam
His food and drink is supplied to him
By the very tree that he lives in

The dingo, looking drawn and thin
Saw there was nothing there for him
Took to the hills at a mighty pace
To get back home before too late

The emu, with his regal frown
Thumped his claw upon the ground
Decided that the things were bad
But he had nothing more to add

The lizard, with his frilly neck
Also came in to see and check
But he backed off without a sound
And found contentment underground

Don't forget the snake, no noise he'd make
As he slithered in, his thirst to slake
A juicy mouse, might be his lunch
A tasty morsel for him to munch

The Tassie devil, with snout held high
Came in to see what he could spy
Though he searches high and low
Nothing there for him to know

The animals then, in ones and twos
Had to decide what they would choose
To drink from the pool, to quench their thirst
Or leave the crock to do his worst

The wise old owl came on the scene
With sight and wisdom, he had seen
The answer to your tale of woe
Take a quick sip and go, go, go.

The Baby Factory

What of the stories that I have been told
The ones that have been from ages old
The cabbage patch was one I'm told
If you want a baby, just moments old

The stork, that flies right through the night
Bringing a baby, wrapped in white
The midwife then comes on the scene
To show the baby, from where it's been

Another of the stories I've been told
When I was a toddler, just a few years old
That mother had swallowed a apple seed
To grow in the tummy after the deed

But now I know, no shadow of doubt
Into the air, I now can shout
For in the picture, you can see
A baby factory, I shout with glee

No more for me those wicked tales
Babies are not from cabbage sales
The answers there for all to see
You buy from the baby factory.

The Barmy Army

The barmy army, loud and crass
Here to see old England crash
Here to help the poms at play
With the cricket test each day

As they shout and sing with glee
All their thoughts and knowledge flee
Perhaps it's 'cause the suns too hot
Or is their talk a lot of rot

England in a five test game
Hasn't won, now that's a shame
But it's army, full of praise
Looks towards their better days

Root sixty six and Broad eight
Blames it on the work of fate
For the toss, against them go
They may have made a better show

The barmy army, mores the shame
Can't follow all the rules of game
Sees the game through just one eye
When the umpire calls out bye

Three down now and two to go
Nature now puts on a show
Sends down rain, even pour
To see the poms take out a draw

One now to go, can they claw back
Or will poor old Joe get the sack
Matters not, for we all know
The Ashes mug will stay below.

The Big Three

Good morning, brothers, how's things today
Looks like a day for fishing, I'd say
The weather looks fine, the sea is so calm
A day's fishing will do us no harm

Well you've had your say on what we could do
I'm just afraid, I've gone down with the flu
So just stand back, just no pushing in
I've also got trouble with my little fin

Now both of you, just hang on a tic
I don't feel well, in fact I feel sick
The weather today is not made for me
So I for one, am not going to sea

Why don't we just go for a dip?
Give our jackets a bit of a zip
Before we waddle off to be with the rest
Back to the pack with all of the pests.

The Blowie

There's a blowfly in the household
And he's getting very bold
He is buzzing when I'm cooking
But stays quiet when I'm looking

I will grab a can of fly spray
Then I'll make that blighter pay
For he's left a little footprint
On my cupboard and my sink

I open up the door, hoping he'll escape
Only thing that happened, I let in his mate
Now there's double trouble in my cosy home
If I don't do something soon, it'l be me who will
    roam

My little four leg canine, a terror and a mate
Had caught himself a blowfly, that he mistakenly ate
He coughed, spluttered and got himself a drink
I wonder what will happen, it's all that I could think

The remaining noisy blowfly, now without a mate
Concerned and worried how his mate had met his fate
Up into the ceiling and escaped through a small crack
And if I read his actions, I'm sure he won't be back.

The Body

This body of mine, that once looked so fine
Oh what a change, with the passing of time
Once looked so healthy, suntanned and groomed
Now it looks flabby, washed out and doomed

Skin no more sun tanned, but blotchy and white
My well slicker's hair, there's a bald head in sight
With eyesight so bright, hearing acute
Now stagger around, and can't hear a coot

The legs that could carry me all through the day
Ache and complain, if I walk then I pay
No bending for me, the back tells me so
The table for meals is the furthers I go

The gall bladders gone, no more would it flow
Heart problems arose, on and off would it go
Doctors have installed a pacemaker to help
It kicks in and helps, this I have felt

Knees need replacing, they're starting to wear
Pains in the side, I think there's a tear
Blood pressure and cholesterol, I check it each day
Your problems old age, is what the doctors do say

The bright side of life, there is one I'm sure
The brain keeps on working, just like a store
It matters not, it knows of my worth
It keeps recording, like it has from my birth.

The Broncos

We have heard the stories of Broncos fighting team
Some would say they're big and strong and mean
But judging by their performance and their little spat
In the State of Origin they performed like pussy cats

They came upon the field to play but got lost upon
    the way
The coach forgot to tell them, just how they ought
    to play
They stood around in clusters, until the blues
    began to score
You could see maroons watching as we, again
    went in for more

It looked just like a rerun of the game of origin one
When maroons stood and watched the blues have
    all the fun
In the days that followed, looks like nothing had
    been learned
With two wins behind them, it's the third game
    that they yearn

The third and final chapter of the game between
    the sides
Will the maroons show courage, as it battles just
    for pride
And turn the little pussies into a pride of roaring
    lions?
The blues, two wins behind them, will keep on
    heading for the line.

The Bugger Died On Me

Returned to my office after lunch and a beer
In barged a woman, her eyes full of tear
"The bugger died and left me" she said
"What do I do now", she asked, nodding her head.

I looked up I'm amazement, to see who was there
There was a blonde, standing right by my chair
I rose up in fear, not knowing what's wrong
Her arms were around me, I had to hang on.

It seemed that her husband, a client of mine
Had died that morning, I don't know what time
"I'll kill him for taking this action on me
His heart gave up working, just after tea".

"I'm lonely and tearful, what should I do?"
"I feel choked up and coming down with the flu"
"I'm tired, lonely and confused as you see
So tell me dear sir, what will happen to me".

Unwrapping my arms from around her slim frame
"I'll represent you", I told her, "I'm good at this game"
She seemed to calm down, and sat on a chair
Asked her to see the will I held there.

It seems that her husband, a man somewhat grim
Quite unprepared for a life without him
Much can be done for the widow there
After a while she'll be breathing clear air.

The matter, you see, is a question of thought
For many see only the now, that is their fault
So let your legacy for kith and kin, held most dear
Be less one of burden and more memory and cheer.

A plan that exists, for the time without us
Is a gift, not a burden, not something unjust
Let the final offer be a world far more certain
Your love they will know, as they pass through that
    curtain.

The Cave Rescue

Tension shows on worried faces
Above the ground and down below
As rescuers fight a two-week battle
A battle, so long and so slow

A soccer team of twelve young lads
Assisted by their worried coach
Trapped in a cave by flooded waters
Through the dark, rescuers approach

Huddled there in cold and darkness
Lack of food and in desperation
News soon leaked of their situation
Became the worry for the nation

A thousand men from many nations
Raced to aid the rescue teams
Helping out in many phases
And in many ways and means

But with the rising waters
And the threat of monsoon rain
The struggle became a race of time
To ease the worry and the pain

The parents stood a daily vigil
Their faces fraught with fear
The worry and frustration
For their children, held so dear

But help, though slow and steady
Has rescued four to date
Then back into the tunnel
To check up on their mate

Four kilometres they had to travel
Through water, mud and slime
To bring the boys back to safety
Along a submerged guiding line

This group of gallant workers
Through mud and drenching rain
Go back into the tunnel
To repeat it all again

Two more trips into the tunnel.
Nine more lads yet to save.
Many heroes in the making
Men so strong and so brave.

As the rescue reaches climax
And the families reunite
Many tired and weary workers
Pleased they won this dreadful fight.

The Chicken

Why did the chicken cross the road?
It's been asked and asked forever
The answer then cannot be told
Without ruffling some feathers

The Rhode Island Red just shook its head
When it's asked to give an answer
The leghorn, white, with comb so red
Played along with lots of banter

The rooster too, who flew the coop
Was reluctant to deliver
An answer that would put a loop
On this puzzle now, forever

The bantam bright, with lots of hype
And his chest poked out before him
I know, I know, with my insight
I will lay it all before you

She crossed the road with lots of flight
With the rooster chasing gamely
In vain she stood, and in a fight
He claimed her, and then left lamely.

The Drought

It was in the summer of 2018
When the rain forgot to fall
And a drought was in the country
It affected one and all

The paddocks dry and barren
Not a blade of grass in sight
And the stockmen of the country
Had a battle and a fight

Hungry and thirsty sheep and cattle
Culled and put up for sale
To tide the farmer over
Should the coming season fail

For months they've been hand feeding
Just to keep their stock alive
And a watch put on the water
As the water levels dive

Then the country made donations
To help the farmer's plight
With many million dollars
To help the farmers in their fight

From Perth they came in numbers
Trucks loaded high with hay
Donated by West farmers
To help farmers find a way

The farmer's now look skyward
And say their prayers for rain
And bless the many donors
That helped them through their pain.

The Early Birds

The kookaburra and the old galah
Started the day with both on par
The kookaburra, with eyes so bright
Gobbled up everything in sight

All that he, the galah could do
Was put am arm around kooka-Sue
Arm in arm they pranced about
Causing kids to leap and shout

Kookaburra laughed to see such fun
Had the children on the run
Mums and Dads were quite impressed
To see the way that kooka dressed

The galah looked tired and over fed
Time for him to rest in bed
The day was great but weather flawed
Rain came on, and down it poured

The Electric Fence

It was early in the morning, few people about
Two elderly people, in a cafe, coffee bout
He turn to her, with a smile on his face
Would you like to have sex as we did our first date?

She's up and she's off, at a terrible pace
He struggles to keep up, but he wins the race
A policeman was sitting at a table nearby,
Hearing , followed them just to keep out an eye

Up comes the skirt, then down with the pants
Backs up to the fence with groans and some pants
Excitement was building, a climax all went
They fell to the ground, exhausted and spent

Recovered and dressed, but shaky and passed
The policeman came out, amazed as he asked
The energy was great, the action supreme
I felt I was having an erotic dream

How do you do it, just what is your drive
The old man just looked while she gave a wave
Our secret, my friend, but don't take offence
We used to back up to an old wooden fence.

The Fight

They laid me down upon a slab
Nothing left of what I had
Which direction will I go?
Up above or down below?

I've got friends in both these places
We'll just see who wins the races
Should I end up with the harp,
Or will the pitchfork be my part?

For my time upon this earth
I have given all my worth
Now the decision isn't mine
Just have to wait the test of time

Now if St Peters at the gate
Will I have to sit and wait
Till He checks my application
To be part of His great nation?

But if I go the other way
Will Old Nick grab my neck and say
I've been waiting for you mate
Get in here, I'll close the gate?

It's not really such a worry
I have time, I'm in no hurry
Let the battle then begin
Just to see who's going to win.

The Foxy One

He waits on the bank of the billabong
Where the saltbush grow, casting shadows long
A burning sun, through a cloudless sky
He's not worried by the occasional fly

A wood duck lands on the placid lake
Waiting there for his lagging mate
The wily fox, with eyes aglow
Just waiting for his chance to go

As the sun dips lower on this heated day
More thirsty animals soon make their way
To sip from the waters in the cooling air
One eye on the water, the other with care

The fox, who'd been waiting for just this time
Looked things over and all seemed fine
One careful leap was all it would take
Or he'd end up within the lake

A red kangaroo came on the scene
Hot and sweaty and quite unclean
Into the water with a mighty bound
Frightened the animals on the ground

The fox, in amazement, leapt and bound
But, alas, no animals to be found
Into the scrub they had hurried fast
Until the noise and panic passed.

The Frog's Eye

The life of the frog, from down in the bog
I see many things from under the log
Here I sit and just wait, to see what's my fate
Will I get breakfast, be it early or late

I cover my eye, to keep out the glare
When I open my eye, there's a moth waiting there
My breakfast supplied, I don't have a care
If things don't work out, my cupboard is bare

My life's not too bad, I don't have to worry
I'm not in a race, I don't have to hurry
If I look for a mate, I'll give her a croak
If she doesn't answer, my heart isn't broke

I'll swim around in my little pond
And of this pool, I'm very fond
It gives me a home, what more can I ask
Don't have to clean up, don't do any tasks

The life of a frog is great, you can see
Nothing to harm or a trouble to me
I'll keep swimming around, enjoying my life
If she won't answer my croak, well who needs a
    wife.

The Ghan

There was movement at the station
From the people gathered waiting
For the train to take them onward
It's the Ghan, that's heading southward

Through the ranges and the foothills
Even dust storms and the rainfalls
It travels onward, night and day
As it wends its southward way

Through its ninety years of travel
With its crew of grit and gravel
Has produced a tourist icon
That the world has settled on

A visit to the Katherine township
We see the way they handle hardship
And the different country scenes
Where the Afghan's had their teams

Overnight we arrive in Alice
A town built like a palace
As we view this town of dreams
Set in such picturesque scenes

At the Overland Telegraph Station
Sent a telegram to a relation
As we watch in awe and wonder
While our message is sent down under

Next to the town they built underground
Coober Pedy, the town we found
Built underground to combat the heat
We consider these buildings a feat

Soon Adelaide we see, the jewel in the south
Our trip is soon over, we all give a shout
With thanks to the crew, and wonderful train
I'm ready to do it all over again.

The Gloucester River

From the Barrington Tops, this river flows
As it progresses, its water grows
Down through the ranges, it travels with glee
Feeling the pleasures of running so free

Through forest and pastures, this river goes
Bubbling or rushing as its mood shows
This river abounds in mullet and perch
With catfish and eels, if only you search

There's boats on the river and fishermen too
Enjoying the waters, so calm and so blue
The banks of the river, willow trees grow
Birds abound on this river, so slow

The river runs through the edge of the town
Down to where the Avon comes down
To continue as one as eastward it flows
Before meeting the Manning, to the ocean it goes.

The Golden Man

Born in Cowra, a town in the bush
Born with a problem that couldn't be fixed
But did it stop him? I answer it, no
And with the world elite, he normally mixed

He's travelled the world, wheelchair in tow
Ready to race, when he's given the go
And proud of the colours, Australian, of course
The green and the gold, always on show

The battles of life, he's handled them all
Encouraged along by family and friends
He's gathered the strength, and will to go on
Content with his lot, is the message he sends

A man with a mission, it's easy to see
Whether the racetrack, or China's Great Wall
Even completed Kakoda's tough trail
Never has taken a back step or fall

Kurt Fearnley, the man who doesn't know fear
Competed against the worlds very best
Winning bronze and silver and many of gold
And at long last, "it's time for a rest"

To Kurt and his family, we give a great cheer
Achievements you've won by courage and grit
And over the years, we'll remember them all
Of the man who used his courage and wit.

The Holy Wall

There's a hole in the wall, it's where one can see
It wasn't put there by Dianne or me
Repair it, you must, said the committee of four
Fix it, we say, or we'll be around at your door

The committee is determined, of this I am sure
I won't be pushed around by them any more
To legal aid, I apply, and like a shot from a gun
They are there to help me, they say it's just fun

The man from Strata, I approached him by phone
He mumbled on and then he let out a groan
I'll check this up and be back to you soon
That's two weeks ago as we approach noon

The hole in the wall, just a half brick in size
One fifty dollars was a quote for this prize
It waits in the ally, so dark and forlorn
To pay out that money, I won't be drawn.

The House on Wheels

I bought myself a house on wheels
Wanted to know just how it feels
Riding the roads way out back
And down a dusty, gravel track

Headed north, along the highway
No more paying the roads tollway
Looking now for greener pasture
As my wheels turn even faster

Passed through Tamworth on the way
Where the country music play
Accompanied by the western bands
There the golden guitar stands

The Queensland border next to cross
I feel that I'm becoming boss
More content in my new home
And contented just to let it roam

Soon we're on the Sunshine Coast
Where we stop for our Sunday roast
View the whales at Harvey Bay
And here to have a two week stay

Townsville next, we set our sight
If we've got the figures right
Green Island there, is calling us
And catch the ferry without a fuss

Mt Isa next, we head out west
Flies and mosquitos become a pest
Scenery now has changed again
The country here needs lots of rain

Southward bound, we head again
Passing the Ghan through a mist of rain
Heading for Alice to replenish stock
Before we continue, to see "The Rock"

Adelaide bound, we continue on
The town where settled the mighty "Don"
Upon the Torrens, the town was laid
And to our journey, it put paid

Our journey's over, we'll settle down
We feel at home in this country town
Our van at home, in a mobile park
And we've had fun on our yearly lark.

The Humble Bra

The ladies needed uplifting help
To keep their lovely figure
If it's too tight they give a yelp
And some want to make it bigger

Many firms have had the bra
With many more invented
Makers come from near and far
Some even have them scented

A movement tried "to burn the bra"
This caused a huge commotion
Most ladies though, way by far
Would not accept this notion

There's Kayser, Joanne and Pretty Looks
That's just a few, there's many more
There all upon the seller's books
And in every hosiery store

There's one though, that has the fame
They went and called it Hestia
I like the way it got the name
"Holds Every Size Tit In Australia".

The Idiot Fringe

Have you seen the people marching
Down the middle of the street
Complaining being locked up
As they chant and fight police?

Just because our country's bleeding
From a virus in the East.
The Delta strain has got us
As we see the thousands sleep

But these loud-mouth lumps of manhood
In their thoughtless bloody mind
Cannot see the trouble caused
By this self-made show of rage

While they fight along for freedom
Others are fighting for their lives
The nursing staff and doctors
Fight to keep the world alive

Could they put their wants behind them
And just suffer for a while?
Giving thoughts to others
Is what this world needs now

It's the courage of the doctors
And their unselfish stand
That will go down in history
Not so the idiot fringe.

The Judgement

He was thrown into the deep end
When asked to judge our verse
For it could have been our writing
Which would have been much worse

But this busy guy from Gloucester
A small hamlet in our north
Put down his pen and paper
And said "I'll give it all it's worth"

Then for days he sat and puzzled
Just to see who's coming first
It was easy for his judgement
To figure just who was worst

He read them all so carefully
Then he read them all again
He was careful with his judgement
To be sure who gets the fame

Stuck the poems upon a blackboard
Placed his hand upon his heart
Picked a missile from the table
And let fly, deftly, with a dart

Now the decision has been final
And the judge has made it clear
Who will be the winners
For computer-pals this year

To Paul, in all his judgement
And his dedication here
We thank him for his input
And give a great big cheer.

The Land We Knew

In this great land, that we call home
Where grass is green and rivers roam
That was until a drought hit here
Been with us now for many a year

The grass browns up, the rivers dry
No rain in sight, no clouds on high
Cattle die, no food on hand
In this, we call the Promised Land

Fires then, tear out our heart
Firefighters doing their part
Hundreds die, many homes lost
To our country, what is the cost?

Soon the sky turns dark and growls
Storm clouds gather and start to prowl
Rain in torrents begin to fall
Upon the ground and river soil

Rivers a banker, towns in flood
Heaviest rains in years, we've had
Rivers running, grasses green
More like the country it has been

Then comes the virus, worldwide flu
Has no respect for me or you
Millions affected, thousands die

Seems little success, whatever they try

This land of ours, this land we knew
Has been affected by the corona flu
Many years, I'm sure we'll see
To make it the world it used to be.

The Mask

It's not just robbers and hoods that use a facial mask
Today you see it in the street and even in the park
They come in many colours, not just black or green
I've seen them in a gentle shade of pink, really
    supreme

There is more news about the humble mask than
In the death and catching of the coronavirus span
In Victoria we are told of the mask and battle there
Where many are reported that a mask they will not
    wear

There are many millions who respect our current law
But there's some that just ignore it, consider it a bore
They are the ignorant, selfish ones who do not give
    a care
To these I give a warning, just be careful and beware

Many jesters, with the wearing of the mask, show a
    flare
Like the man who wore nothing but a mask, you
    know where
Or the chap who made a mask from his wife's
    rejected bra
Of the arguments about it, this is the brighter side,

by far.

The Mighty Hunter

Up in the mountains, in rarefied air
It's nought but a trickle but still it is there
Amongst ferns and bracken, it's there to be seen
The Hunter was born in this distant scene

Two hundred K's away from its mouth
Heading down slowly, south-east by south
It's only a trickle of fresh water there
Picks up volume as it travels with care

Passing towns and village, as it makes its pace
Heading off eastward, as if in a race
Through vineyards and gardens and riverside trees
Assisted along with the afternoon breeze

This river of ours, a slow-moving stream
A picturesque scene, you see in a dream
But let the rains come, the river will swell
Out over the banks, the farmers will tell

Through tree lands and pasture, our river flows
Over culverts, under bridges that river goes
It's heading now east, the ocean to meet
A long way it has travelled, but it won't be beat

It's widened out, on reaching the coast

The best of the best, it's really no boast
Then out into the ocean, it travels with glee
The aim of the river is to be part of the sea.

The Mighty Lion

Is it a headache or is it in shame
Poor old Leo, he's feeling the pain
His days are over of roaring in glory
This is the tail and end of his story

For years his roar has been heard
By the deer and the antelope herd
Now they just stare at this beast
He can't catch them and have a big feast

His reign is over, a new king is there
Poor old Leo, his cupboard is bare
Behind the paw, there's tears in his eyes
All he has left is a bed and bye byes

Don't feel sorry for him, his time has been long
We'll play him some music and sing him a song
The law of the jungle, relates now to him
His body is tired and his eyes are so dim.

The Mobile Man

I saw a man upon his phone
On the verandah of his home
I've seen him on his phone before
I guess I'll see him there some more

I passed this way another day
He waved, as I went on my way
But with his phone, upon his ear
I wonder if the receptions clear

A rainy day, I had a peek
He's on his phone another week
A cuppa on the windowsill
I wonder just who'll pay the bill

Hasn't moved from there, I'm sure
Since I saw him there before
But from today I'm leaving home
Around the world I plan to roam

Ten years on, I'm back again
Looking through the sleet and rain
Saw the man's mobile phone
Upon a heap of human bone.

The Mouse Within

There's a pesky little mouse
Somewhere within my house
I don't see him very often
But he leaves his little dropping

I will have to set a trap
For this wily little chap
Or perhaps I'll get a cat
But I'm not so fond of that

It will really be a pity
If I have to get a kitty
For my bird within his cage
Would attack me, in its rage

So I have myself this worry
And perhaps I shouldn't hurry
To exterminate this blighter
Who's become a little fighter.

Then and Now

We have these nice, new, toilets now
But I remember when and how
We'd visit the dunny out the back
Through a winding garden track

No privacy we had those days
We'd be seen, when people gaze
Going in or coming out
There were usually folk about

The nightsoil men would come at night
And take the pan, oh what a sight
But it's the smell that follows it
That leaves one in an awful fit

But now today it's kept inside
Water flushes now, with pride
No one there to spy on you
As you go to your water loo

Science with its latest notion
Sends our flushes into the ocean
Leaves our toilets nice and clean
Toilet smells now like a dream.

The Odd Bunch

Who was it said "imagination is dead"
When I can see a young baby, no head
There's a body there too, just coming through
But a hand in the way, it's so true

When I look at the top, it's a carrot I spy
But could change into hair, in a flash of an eye
With the magic of my imagination
To match up with the world's inflation

It's an odd bunch we are, but we could go far
As we look, from the side of "the bar"
For the figure in sight, we could put up a fight
As the carrot goes down in one bite.

The Old Homestead

Winter sets in on the place once called home
Where cattle went free, as they used to roam
Stockmen once rode through valleys and hills
Herding their stock, while showing their skills

Many years have passed since people lived here
Once it was happy and filled with good cheer
But drought and depression were with us for years
With costs and prices reduced us to tears

A journey back home to visit and see
Brought back the hardship and what had to be
The house is still standing, doors are a miss
Memories abound when I look at this

Snow has fallen, as it used to be
Rot and desertion is all I can see
When summer returns, grass will be green
I'll go home, contented with what I have seen.

The Outback

It was a wind created hell
Somewhere in Australia's outback
That lifted both sand and fine shell
On the swag man's face and backpack

Desert of sand ranges, lying
Among salt bush, stunted and dry
The wind sending grasses flying
And sending them up into the sky

The swagman, with eyes red and sore
Fed up with flies that surround him
Pushed on with eyes to the fore
Dreaming of a river to swim

He plods on with single of purpose
Assured with his direction and time
Along with a few little curses
For tomorrow will certainly be fine

Another few miles in this dust storm
He shall stop for his billy of tea
And rest there till the coming of dawn
Knowing there's no paying of fees

Weariness blacked out his worries
He slept like a man in a trance
Awoke to the rumble of lorries
And viewed then a difference expanse

The sun had peeped through the treetops
Presenting a new type of day
The swaggie still has a few stops
So he's up and off on his way

The morning was bright but chilly
He still had a long way to run
Up with his swag and his billy
And heads off out into the sun.

The Painter

Across the painter's canvas
Across the painter's mind
There's many a painting waiting
To make a debut there

The painter, in his glory
Works at terrific speed
To get his ideas on there
Before his paint has dried

His meals almost forgotten
As he paints away with glee
Be it morning, noon or evening
It's there for all to see

There's movement in the household
Another painting done
Time to be with family
With the setting sun.

The Rainbow

I gazed upon a clouded sky
A shower of rain just passing by
And left behind a beautiful sight
A rainbow with its glorious light

As I stood and watched this sight
I felt that all in my life was right
Red, orange, yellow, green
Blue, indigo and violet seen

Many words are said in praise
Of myths and tales in many ways
Then as the children's stories tend
A bucket of gold at rainbows end

I think of red in many shades
Orange as the daylight fades
Yellow for an early morn
And grasses green, it is the norm

Blue is for the cloudless skies
Indigo, the colour that's prized
And violet for the flowers that grow
To take the name of the violet glow

But as I watch, it fades away
I'll wait until it comes, another day
To glory at this sight I see
I hope it makes a better me.

The Rain in Spain

The rain in Spain falls long and clear
More rain they've had than just one year
In just hours, all this rain had fell
Like a scene straight out of hell.

The waters rush, the barriers break,
The town becomes a massive lake.
Men and women washed away,
Death and destruction here to stay.

Roads and houses washed away,
Cars piled up like a massive highway,
Rescuers around in boats and skips,
Water covers the whole township.

Throughout the week the mud lays thick,
Help is needed for aged and sick.
Finally then the army's called in,
With much ado, noises and din.

People not happy, no help from the top.
When will the worry of mud really stop?
Residents are angry, no help can they get,
Just worry and hardship mingled with fret.

The Ride

She sat upon an old black nag
Between her lips, a burnt-out fag
With legs stuck out on either side
All ready for a bumpy ride

The air is crisp, with frost around
Covering the hard baked ground
A final check that all was right
The look on the face, she's had a fright

The horse takes off at a gentle pace
He'll not hurry, no need to race
A dog lets out a mighty yell
The horse took off, she nearly fell

He raced on, like Phar lap would
Through the gate, into the wood
A frightened cry soon was heard
I'll not quote it word for word

Soon we see her limping back
Leading the horse along the track
No more horses, she will ride
She'll walk to regain her shattered pride.

The Rivers Run

Across the coastal plain, across the mountain range
Rain came down in torrents, the worst of weather change
Floods across the coast lands, and rivers run amok
Of the western rivers, they face the same bad luck

The waters of the Murray, westward as it flows
Consuming all before it, as the water grows
Town and cities scurry, to build their levee banks
With sandbags, heavy tractors, even army tanks

For weeks the waters rumble, spreading out with ease
Flooding towns and homestead, toppling many trees
Isolating townships, with roads now out of sight
The people of the Murray, view the sight with fright

Many weeks along the Murray, the turbid water flows
Until it reaches Wentworth, where another river grows
The Darling joins the Murray, more force upon the land
The army joins the forces and try to make a stand

Two months the waters travelled, with no relief in sight
Into another State it flows, to continue with its fight
The South Australian townships, many weeks they've tried
Preparing for a monster and overturn its tide

The river, still running strongly, now heading out
    to sea
Leaves behind a record for generations to see
With towns and cities in its wake, lots of work at
    best
While the Mighty Murray once more lays at rest.

The Scorpion

A scorpion walked with tail held high
A warning to those passing by
A message there that should be read
Or one could end up stone-cold dead

He worries not, for he is free
As long as others let him be
But if you like to try your luck
Well then push on with lots of pluck

He met up with a snake one day
And made the slithery creature pay
He laid a sting behind the ears
And struck him dead, so it appears

The scorpion then went on his way
Was no need for him to stay.
He knew that they'd not dally him
Or risk a barb beneath the skin

He's roamed enough for him today
Tomorrow is another day
Let those that know, a warning thus
Get on with life, no need to fuss.

The Senior

For forty years we've been there for you
With many stories, all so true
Of world events, and local too
When feeling well, or feeling blue

And as the years drift quickly past
We know that forty is not our last
So we carry on with all that's new
To bring the very best to you

A travel section, for the wise
Showing you good travel buys
Whether it be overseas
Or catching a local ocean breeze

For grey nomads, there's many tales
Of tours they've done, or watching whales
And if they've seen it all before
They're off again, looking for more

We finish off our forty years
There' no need for shedding tears
We'll be back for all we're worth
And give forty-one a brand new birth.

The Snowy Men

There's been many stories written
There's been many stories told
Of the men from Snowy River
They're the boldest of the bold

Through the wildest of the mountains
Up and down the mountain side
You would find these willing horsemen
Ever ready for their ride

They were a band of hardy horsemen
Born and bred in country towns
Knew the value of their horses
Loved the battle and the sounds

They've had cattle in the mountains
For at least a hundred years
And it seemed it would be forever
They had no worries or no fears

Then their life style is really shattered
When the government takes a hand
And advises all and sundry
That their actions have been banned

Now their lives are torn and shattered
And the results they can't defend
So for the riders of the mountain
It's to be a saddened end.

The Spider

There's a spider on the wall
But he's headed for a fall
As he dangles from a cord
On his way onto a board

When she spied this interloper
She cried "it's not a happy joker"
So for Mortein she makes a dash
Then the spider gets a splash

The spider, sprayed and splattered
And his web, it's now so mattered
As he twists and turns and battles
As his body gets the rattles

Then a plunge, as he goes floor-ward
She, in haste, also goes forward
Just to see her win, in battle
As she lets out a triumphant cackle

The spider, now quite unsighted
She feels that she's been blighted
So now she's off to bed
Poor old spider must be dead

But on the following morning
Just as the sun is dawning
I see spider near her chair
With all legs up in the air.

The Story of Morse

Many stories have been told
Of messages sent, in days of old
Some were sent by signal smoke
While others think it's all a joke

But ask the Indian, brave and strong
If he ever got the message wrong
When he would let his smoke stream go
Upon the wind, he'd let it flow

Until a man named Samuel Morse
Came upon the world in force
To use his dots and dashes code
And took the world into his fold

A message then would fly around
Over water and over ground
Conveying news to those at home
From the ones who loved to roam

In times of war, the signals went
Across the world, the news is sent
Then like a flash, the answers back
Upon the sounder in the shack

In war and peace, the message sped
With vital news, that's quickly read
That was until nineteen sixty-two
When Morse had died, like systems do

But we, the old, of Morse men know
That Morse to us is still on show
And if you should hear the click and clack
You will know that Morse is back.

The Talk

I did a talk at Anglicare
With many people listening there
To all the things I had to say
I hope they all enjoyed the day

It started off with morning tea
Then I made a silent plea
That I could get my stories through
And make them interesting for you

Mary there in a comfy chair
Thomas there with a cross to bear
While all the others sit and wait
To see what will be their fate

The stories now, are coming fast
Of things of now and in the past
The stories told, I swear are true
As I relate them here for you

A poem or two, a joke in here
I hope it's what you want to hear
Sit back and rest and let it be
And leave the worries up to me.

The Todd

The Todd is in the news again
This time with pouring rain
From side to side the river burst
While the locals watch and curse

The Todd regatta, in the past
A classic in its class
Was run along the dry river bed
Through mud and dust of red

The country now with flooding rain
Stops traffic and the train
While the inland town of Alice Springs
Talk of floods and rescue things

A hundred mils in just one day
Is what the bureau say
They haven't seen a sight this way
Since Noah had his day.

The Traveller

Across the turbid waters, across the sandy loam
My love from distant countries, is finally heading home
For months I've been awaiting, the return from distant shores
I will greet her warmly, with open arms and doors

She headed off to England, with rellies there to see
A quick trip on to Ireland, across the Irish Sea
Before her trip to Europe, with Euros in her hand
To see the land of Holland, or is it the Netherland?

A letter from her briefly, to say that she was fine
But on the rush, as always, not one for wasting time
The coach has reached the border of yet another place
Then off to see what's offered, with a smile upon her face

Her time is passing quickly, like the moving sands of time
But with her luck and courage, I'm sure she'll turn out fine
The days and weeks of travel have now turned into months
With only days remaining, it's souvenirs that she hunts

So now I am preparing, for the day that she comes home
   And wonder, as I sit here, if in the future she will roam
But as she sees the washing and housework still undone
Will she have me riding into the setting sun?

The Trip

The ship has left its mooring, the sun sets in the west
While the harbour master's tugboat, is working at
 its best
Our sky has turned to amber, the suns last final fling
The clouds have turned to darkness, night covers
 everything

The lights within the harbour, twinkle as they shine
Our ship is headed eastward, across the darkened
 brine
Night has overtaken, the day that was so fine
And with the early morning, another day we'll find

The ship has changed directions, northward across
 a placid sea
We wait for our tomorrow, to see what's there to see
A long day we have travelled, and tired are we all
With the break of morning, we're ready for a ball

Night has turned to morning, the sun now peeping
 through
The sky above the cloud line, shows a mass of
 azure blue
A gentle breeze is blowing, across a calm blue sea
White caps on the water, it's there for all to see

Onward, ever onward, the north is calling us
We'll reach there in the morning, without undue rush
We've reached our destination, robust and fully fed
Todays a day for sight-seeing, then return to ship
 and bed.

The Tucker Box

I was heading off to Albury
Down the Hume for miles and miles
Had my tools and working kit
As well as all my files

Got as far as Gundagai
Where the dog sat on his box
I wondered what the story was
As I walked out in my sox

I saw a fellow sitting there
He looked like he might know
But when I asked about it
Got a bleary-eyed straight "no"

I looked around for the "info" store
But, afraid, it was lacking too
Then came upon a little lad
He looked to be about two

He told me what his story was
As best as he could be
So I will relate it now, to you
Just the way it was told to me

The dog had worked with a drover
In the box was the drover's eats
The driver, he got called away
With the dog to protect his keeps

The drover wasn't seen again
And the dog laid down and died
Then they built this statue
For the faithful dog that tried.

So still the dog sits on the tucker box
Nine miles from Gundagai, our story goes
That faithful dog, he sat to wait
But his master never shows.

The Voice of the Sea

The voice of the sea, speaks to the soul
But only to those, who dare to be bold
It roars from the deep, a voice to be heard
But only to you, who understands its word

It lays down there deep, as if it's asleep
Yet the waves, up above, they play or they weep
The whales and the Dolphins, display their own grace
While the small flying fish, run their own race

The turtle, at home, on a wave, it floats by
You won't crack his shell, as hard as you try
Then shark hurries past, he's after a feed
A school of sardines is the thing that he needs

A hurricane arrives, to churn up the seas
It races along, no more just a breeze
Sends out a challenge, to the voice down below
Then puts on its own terrible show

The voice from the deep, awakes in a rage
To study the scene, just like an old sage
Set off the waves, into a mountainous sea
Attempting to make this old hurricane flee

The fight carries on, the sea and the wind
Calm will return when this battle does end
Then once more, for those who do care
The voice of the sea will ring in the air.

The Waiting Room

I sit upon a padded chair
Amongst the nervous patients there
And listen to the coughs and groans
As well as those upon their phones

A woman there with long black hair
With tattoos showing everywhere
A bandage wrapped around her head
She might be better off in bed

We heard a loud and retching sound
Then see her fly by, toilet bound
Soon she returns, a shattered wreck
With a napkin wrapped around her neck

A wheelchair patient, next in line
He looks healthy, fit and fine
Yet upon his face, he wears a frown
And dressed within a dressing gown

We've waited here for quite some time
The nurse has said that all was fine
But then she said "just wait a tick,
I'm afraid our doc just called in sick".

The Way We Were

I ask you friend, do you remember when
The way we were, when we were young, back then
I remember well, how things were done
Almost, that is, since my life begun

Bread was delivered right to your door
Not a sliced loaf at door or in store
Milk delivered, a glass bottle was used
Then washes and returned for its reuse

The way we were, I tell you friend
Today it would turn you around the bend
No T V nor mobile, just a phone on the wall
A voice at the end of your telephone call

The way we were, we had a good life
Some children, friends and a loving wife
Monies not great, but plenty of feed
What more could be asked, any more it is greed.

The Wedding

She got an invite "To you know where"
But cried "I've got nothing to wear
I'm so embarrassed, I can't go
Oh dear, Oh dear what a blow

Perhaps Her Royal Highness, in her grace
May have some rag in her place
That she may scrape up and perhaps lend
So that I, in my haste, may attend

The love of my life is Harry dear
But think that I've lost, mores the fear
Yet I must go, and for him to see
Just what he has done to me

Charles and Camilla, I know will be there
A dress of white, I'm sure she'll wear
William's son and daughter bright
To walk down the aisle, is just right

I could mix with the guests, one and all
Providing that I accept the call
Then watch the marriage of Harry and Meg
Oh what a dream, this I beg

The night draws on, the thunder peels
I open my eyes, I know how it feels
I've had a bad night, or so it would seem
For I've woken up from a very bad dream.

The World

This world of ours that we call home
With many countries for us to roam
Where grass is green and rivers run
In this place, Earth, beneath the sun

The ocean waves, to join the lands
To make the pristine ocean sands
With rain to make the forest grow
And let the mighty rivers flow

The sunrise breaks in early morn
Sending colours across the dawn
With the sun's movement, as in flight
And settles down to sleep at night

A gentle breeze is seen on high
Chasing clouds across the sky
When the black clouds come in sight
Rain and wind put up a fight

This world of ours, through many ages
Changed the ways, in many stages
Lava spread across the ground
Where green grass will soon be found

This land of ours with its motion
Churns the seas and the ocean
In the sun the country bask
Is there more that we can ask.

The Yellow Room

I've travelled far across the Globe
Saw Cape Town and been to Robe
The Golden Gate and Tower Bridge
And also towns like Lightning Ridge

The Floating Markets in Vietnam
Also used South Africa's Rand
Climbed the heights of China's Wall
Did this all without a fall

Went along to see St Pauls
Even saw Niagara Falls
Spent a night upon a barge
On the river, out of Prague

The Panama was quite a sight
Hong Kong markets really a fight
Peru and Bolivia next to shine
Also on the Holland America line

On a boat in Halong Bay
T'was in dongs I had to pay
Sailed on oceans, big and small
I think that I have covered all

Hotels, motels, guest house too
And I am really telling you
Even on my honeymoon
I never been in a yellow room.

They're Racing

The starter saw the racers off
The good, the bad and even toffs
But one has shown the rest clean heels
As off he races, and without appeals

A strong wind blowing into the face
But has no effect against the pace
It seems the legs have more than two
As he races off, into the blue

The loose sand moves as he flies by
With head held high, towards the sky
The finish line is next we see
Beside a peaceful, azure sea.

Things in Life

There's things in life that are hard to explain
Be it simple or complex, it's all just the same
Why do we do it, or why is it done
Is it because we all live under the sun?

As a lad, was told, there's a man in the moon
Now they tell us, we'll be walking there soon
Why, I ask, would you want to be there?
Life on earth, we're just needing fresh air

Volcanos and earthquakes, why do they act
A vulcanologist may give us the facts
Tsunami is another, I don't understand
Destruction abounds when it takes a hand

Conservationists tell us, the earth's in a state
A collapse is expected, if we keep up this rate
Those who can change it, don't seem in a race
They move along at a stop and start pace

When all's said and done, little is done
There's little to laugh at, such little fun
A pandemic it seems, can't make us gel
It looks much like "we're heading for hell".

Things Most Missed

I'm often asked about my life
And what I miss the most
You'll not believe the tale I tell
And this, no idle boast

I throw some stuff into the bin
Or at least that's what I try
Half the stuff goes in the bin
But the rest just passes by

I pick it up and try again
This time from closer range
It really seems to move itself
As if I have the mange

I open mail and put the stuff
Into the bin, by hand
But do you believe, it's stuck to me
You can see it as I stand

I place the bin close by my chair
This time I must be right
I kicked the bin right over
For I had received a fright

The bin and its contents
Were strewn across the floor
I had to tidy up the mess
Then tossed it out the door.

This Body

Within this body, a spirit does dwell
Or that is the story our ministers tell
It is the driving force, kept well within
This human body, a temple for him

As through our life, we travel as one
Through strife and worry and even fun
Your body and mine, when the ring of the bell
Our spirits the one goes to Heaven or Hell

Our worn-out bodies, no use, I am bound
Will end up as ashes, or deep underground
So work for your spirit, help with his plight
Be it heaven or hell, may he have a good flight.

Threatened Species

Threatened species are the worries of the world
In China lives the panda, in colours, black and white
While in Borneo we have the gorilla big and brave
Oceans hold the blue whale, such an awesome sight

The koala in Australia, a cuddly little thing
New Zealand has the kiwi, the funny little bird
Our crocodile, in Australia, doesn't give a smile
While the Tasmania tiger has been missing a while

The platypus with flat tail and a bill
And their young that come from an egg
Placed on a list of those who'll be missed
Together with so many more.

I've told you about, and you're not now in doubt
Of the passing of species untold
But the one that I fear, still on that list
Is the one in clothes at the top.

Through a Window

Through the window of a moving train
I watch the gentle falling rain
Making scenes upon the glass
As we, hurriedly, go past

Then a break up in the sky
No more rain, we've passed it by
To see a scene of mountains, blue
And waterfalls cascading too

But soon the scene has changed again
We're passing through the western plain
With sheep and cattle grazing there
Gathered there without a care

A station now, we do not stop
We see some 'roos, they're on the hop
Scared no doubt, by our whistle blast
As they take off, moving fast

For miles and miles, the country's bare
Can't even see a long-eared hare
A shade of blue up in the sky
While a pair of eagles swoop and fly

So now our journey nears its end
There's things for me to do and tend
The curtain falls on the window's view
I must be ready to depart too.

Thunderbolt's Cave

I remember a time, and I remember it well
If you give me the time, of it, I will tell
When a group of us lads, just boys, but all brave
Went to investigate "Thunderbolt's" cave

At the edge of the town, stood a range to behold
Where rumour abounds and we had to be bold
For we had been told that his ghost still roamed
We were eager but wary, our nerves were well honed

The day soon arrived, as we head for that cave
Loaded with torches to keep us all brave
The stories told of this outlaw's deeds
Fresh in our mines like fast growing seeds

The moment arrived, who's first to go in
Quiet there fellows, what is that din
Trembling with fear, we're ready to run
Then we decide it's only a drum

Courage restored, we're in with a rush
Which of my mates can I really trust?
My torch has gone out, I'm needing help
Just at that moment someone lets out a yelp

Our courage all gone, only panic remains
We head for the light, out onto the plains
The cave can remain Thunderbolts domain
We're heading for home no more do we roam.

Tiger at Sea

The blue of the sky, reflects on the ocean
While waves roll along, in a gentle motion
A world at peace, or that's what it seems
Yet under the water the fish are in teams

But down in the deep, the scourge of the sea
The tiger is waiting, the fish turn and flee
He swims on past, no interest he shows
Yet he'll eat when his ready, the little one knows

A flash as he turns, like lightning he goes
To escape from those, the ones he calls foes
Just when he's ready, he'll go for his feed
But only take those, to satisfy his need

The water churns as he attacks
There's nothing slow, weak or lax
Movement smooth as he moves in
Using tail and mouth and even fin

Then as the frenzy settles down
No turmoil now, not even sound
The tiger continues on his way
With nature's way, some have to pay.

Time

The sands of time are moving fast
As I sit here, thinking of the past
When as a boy, I'd laugh and play
Put off things for another day

No T.V. then to see world's life
Did not get in too much strife
An uncomplicated life we had
Our daily strife was not too bad

Our schooling then, we had the best
Always passed our yearly tests
Adverbs, nouns and conjunctions too
With our learning, time just flew

Forty-eight hours a week, we toiled
End of day, we're sweat and soiled
A bath at night to ease the pain
Tomorrow, we do it all again

Retirement comes, life's work is done
Days have come to sit in the sun
The old world's gone, a new one's here
I look ahead with doubt and fear

Laptops with us and mobile phones
I look at them, with grunts and groans
And wonder what, is the world in doom
When I see man walk on the moon

My life has had a rocky run
I wonder, as I sit out in the sun
In a hundred years what will it be?
I'm sure I won't be here to see.

Titanic Sleeps

Across the oceans, dark and deep
Many ships, on seabed, sleep
Titanic is the classic one
Where people sailed for sea and sun

Titanic sailed from British shores
With much fanfare and great applause
To United States for its port of call
Until fate arrived for its fatal fall

An iceberg came upon the scene
Floating on the sea of green
Passengers on the stricken ship
Into the lifeboats rather quick

SOS, the calls go out
To any ship that's hereabout
Many lives, that day were lost
Of human life, what was the cost

A hundred years and more, it's been
Since the Titanic last was seen
And then at last, a wreck was found
Asleep upon where it was drowned.

Today / Tomorrow

Tomorrow is another day
We often hear the pundits say
But if it's like the one I had
I'm sure that it would make me sad

The morning started warm and clear
I gave a little hollow cheer
But when I turned the shower on
No hot water, it's all gone

My shower then, was not for me
I'll settle for a cup of tea
Toast and jam then was my aim
But then I had a tummy pain

So off to work I had to go
Thought I'd better make a show
The motor then let out a woosh
Then I needed a little push

At long last I made it there
Only to find the cupboard bare
A note upon the outer door
This business closed forever more

Off to home I sadly went
Found out all my money's spent
Took myself off to my bed
And knew now why I'd never wed.

Today's Weather

Woke up this morning and all things seemed well
Looked out the window, was a wind there from hell
It blew so hard that trees bent over in pain
Now it looks like it's going to rain

The clouds so black but the white lining shows
Chased along by the wind which still blows
But the sun battles on, to show he's supreme
Attacks the clouds like a vacuum machine

In no time at all, the sun wins the fight
Yet still has a battle, with the wind in his sight
He's roamed these skies for many a year
Attacks all the seasons, showing no fear

The hands of the clock keep hurrying on
While up in the skies, rolls on our red sun
Nature, you'll find if you read in the book
That old man sun, after us, he will look.

Touring

I have sailed upon the oceans, and on the seven seas
Have seen the world around us, just taken when I
    please
We'd fly off to the Pacific, a hula there, we'd do
Then scuba diver Suva to see the ocean's zoo

Headed off to Europe, spending Euros by the score
A camel ride in Egypt and the pyramids, we saw
A tiny boat we boarded, down the Nile we slowly
    drift
Then it's back to Cairo, for a dinner at the Ritz

In Greece we saw the islands, taken in by Rhodes
Liked the Trevi fountain, but not the mating crowds
Rode the famous gondolas, saw the leaning tower
Climbed the Eiffel Tower while dodging local shower

Crossed the bridge from Europe to Asia, in the rain
Then it's on to China, in a big jet plane
We travelled one the fast trains, 240k's an hour
And wonder of the chaos, if it should lose its power

There're many stories to be told, of travels near or far
Of things we've seen and heard, while on our travel
    card
So if you have the and really have the care
Call in and see me, in my humble rocking chair.

Tranquility

Across the waters, calm and deep
On the bank where willows weep
Mountains come down to the sea
Where people live calm and free

Distant mountains stand on show
Covered then in winters snow
Summertime it's lush and green
Where native animals can be seen

On the placid waters show
How the distant forest grow
And how man has blended in
On this peaceful setting then.

Travelled Out

Travel book between my knees
Looking for some place to flee
Been tied up some weeks or so
Think I'll give the world a go

Not the time to go to Turkey
Fires, floods and weather murky
Too many Japs in Tokyo
On the river Rhine, go with the flow

Johannesburg with riots flaring
India, it takes some bearing
Afghanistan with wars ongoing
Antarctica shores, there is no flowing

In China you can be charged with spying
Russia I'd be charged with lying
Try America then, no it's too boring
France of course, there'd be no scoring

My book has fallen while I'm dreaming
Must go online and do some streaming
Lost me urge to leave my home
With covid then I'm best alone.

Tree Love

Love, I find, comes in all sorts and sizes
Some start off young, with other it rises
The story I tell of two trees entwined
Letting their passions to really unwind

It's been many years in the making
Now it seems she's there for the taking
Gone is the shyness, held in his heart
While she is willing to do her best part

Arms and legs entwined with embrace
Neither of them are into a race
Ignoring the birds and leaves that are there
To each other, they lay themselves bare

I'll leave them enraptured, tangled in love
Blue is the sky, way up above
A picture perfect, is the sight that I see
They won't be interrupted, even by me.

Tribute to Pandemic Medicos

To the doctors, nurses and ambulance drivers
It's thanks to you we've so many survivors.
A pandemic with us, which knows no mercy
Attacked the aged and feeble firstly,

Then delta came, to spread much worse.
When doctors, nurses became the first
To front this curse, with all your training
But saps your strength and leave you draining.

The ambo's became the new front lines
Shuttling patients with first signs.
Doctors, sisters and nursing crew
Do the tasks they learned to do.

Hours, days turn into years,
Still we live in constant fears.
Just the jabs and you between us
You carry on, no blame, no fuss.

You show to us your love and devotion
Combining with some deep emotion,
As you carry on each day.
It's for the Lord and you we pray.

Troll On

Today we see a troll in pose
Standing with a big fat nose
We can see upon that spot
Where the birds have made a drop

Standing there so brave and bright
Making quite a pretty sight
With his flag of country shown
While standing on a shelf of stone

If by chance you should go by
A photo there, if you should try
Or maybe on the river run
You could have some water fun

He'll be there for many days
People come to see and pays
Happy with the sight and pose
And of the way our world goes.

Trolls

Trolls by the dozens, we found
Some at large while others were bound
Colours and shapes, whatever you wish
One with a pole, trying to fish

Appearing to hop from rock to rock
Many, it seemed, ready to drop
Norway is where these little ones are
Some perched up on top of a bar

When the river runs high, washes them clean
Many I've seen, washed down the stream
Some appear in their National flag
Others it seems just want to brag

Certain I am and this I am sure
Turn down a corner, there's many more
The city is full of these little trolls
Much more exciting than cuddling dolls.

Trouble is Me

Trouble seems to follow me, I don't know how it is
Perhaps I have a magnet that's been cleverly
    concealed
Or is it just that lady luck has looked the other way
When I do the things I do, they have always been
    revealed

When I was just a little lad, t'was me that got the
    blame
Though I wore my halo high, it didn't stop the rot
The fingers on the bony hands always point at me
Although I'm not an angry sole, my blood was
    running hot

When I attended primary school, I tried to change
    it all
But soon I found I'd carried on, Jonah came to
    school
And like the apple barrel, I was the bad one in the lot
Again I tried to change it and I acted up the fool

With my schooling over, and I survived it all
I turned my hand to working, to earn a buck or two
It's amazing how it happens, it wasn't meant to be
But there I was working at the Taronga Park zoo

I thought that I was clever, working in the park
Even I know that the animals cannot point
With food and water flowing, the gates securely
    locked
I can't get into trouble, if I work around this joint

We've heard about that finger, the fickle finger of fate
That finger's pointing, and it's pointing right at me
The deer got in the lion's den, the lions ate them all
I'm looking for another job, but not a zoo, you see

When I go to heaven, for I've done my time in hell
Will St Peter greet me, or turn me down below
In this world of uncertainties, it's really hard to tell
I guess I have no option but to let the forces flow.

Trump Trumped

The wind has gone from Mr. Trump
We'll have to get the man a pump
To inflate him, like he used to be
So that his fans, he'll be able to see

The face we see, when he comes out
A scowl upon his lips, which pout
All his gust and zoom have blown
Just what a man is what is shown

The White House now, no trumpets blast
Yet Trumps are there, but not to last
They wait for Joe to fill the place
And show that he has won the race

American people, both black and white
Have been thanked for their great fight
Awaiting now, a change of rule
Followed now by a tight schedule.

Trusted Friend

My true and trusted friend, we've forty years
    together
Travelled the world, seen the sights, ignoring the
    weather
Now as the years get higher and the time get faster
We sit and watch the world go by and ready for our
    Master

As the evening shadows lengthen and the stars
    begin to shine
While the shadows on the water reflects the
    passing of the time
For the days are getting longer and the nights are
    in decline
While the night birds send their calling that
    tomorrow should be fine

The lights in the distance send a message of their
    own
And the rumble of the traffic is a constant
    humming tone
While the moon is peeping over a distant mountain
    range
Sending tongues of moonbeams right across the
    whole terrain

There's a stillness settled over the meadows and the field
And the horses amble onward until finally they yield
Then to listen to the motor of a vehicle, highly powered
While the dog, as if in terror, in his kennel he has cowered

Still the night has more to offer, as it turns a darker shade
Then the clouds and wind together, set out to make raid
To cover up the moonlight and play havoc with the stars
And tries to send off torrents on the unsuspecting cars

But the moon has overpowered both the wind and then the clouds
And the brightness of the evening has scattered all the shrouds
While the lovers watch in wonder at the phases of the moon
And the night will turn into morning and alas, it's all too soon.

Truth

I am a politician,
I'm working very hard
To represent my people
Of this I'm very glad

I meet many varied people
This causes lots of stress
I got to many functions
Where I wear my formal dress

Then when it comes to voting
I am there amongst the rest
And cast my vote on something
And I give it all my best

Our party room gets heated
As we discuss it all
Yet when it's finally settled
It's to the pub and have a ball

Then when my term is over
It makes me rather sad
For in my time in sessions
I've handled truth so very bad.

Two Cat Ladies

This is the story I wanted to tell
About two cat ladies, and pussies as well
One cat was white, black tail and toes
Other is brown with white legs and nose

The brown one is Charlie, a male to the core
While Meekah, a female, but she's not a bore
The cat ladies are friends, talk every day
This can't be said of the cats, I'm afraid

Charlie comes out, to try and make friends
Meekah, in turn, it's Charlie she sends
Charlie will give a hiss then he will go
While the little "white miss", her rear end on show

The cat ladies still talking, eyes on the cats
They don't want them to have their little spats
These two little furies don't like one and other
Content are they, just to be with their "mother"

So cat ladies beware, when your cats are about
When they get together, be ready to shout
With fight in the air, on who do you bet
The one who laughs longest, the family vet.

Two Frogs

Two frogs out for the day, dressed in their Sunday best
Sun was shining, day was great, thinking that they were blessed
One was wearing his heart on his sleeve, the other taking snaps
Until a magpie flew by, taking the frog's little cap

Without a cap they hurried on, to see what they could see
All went well until one was stung by a passing bumble bee
He croaked and croaked then croaked some more
For the beautiful life that they had sort, suddenly became a bore

Back to the pond the little frogs went, to end their busy day
Into the muddy water they flopped, with not a thing to say
Submerged in the mud the little frogs played
Contented and that's where both of them stayed.

Two Little Birds

Upon my garden fence, I saw, a tiny jenny wren
The black and brown of feathers, seen in this tiny glen
She twisted, turned and fluttered, presumed all was swell
Until a Willy Wagtail flew in there as well

He was dressed in tucks and tails, in black and white, he's set
Jenny in her frock of brown, not ready for him yet
She flicked her tail this way and that, as pretty as can be
Watching Willy all the way, to see what he could see

Willy, on the garden post, let go a tune or two
Then leapt into the air, a sky of brilliant blue
Landing on the garden rail, quite close to little Jenny
He sang a further song to her, but she's not helping any

Dusted down his wedding suite, while eyeing off the maiden
The chances now of winning, appears that they are fading
Off he flies, with a farewell loop, green pastures are calling
He'll try his luck with a wagtail lass, then see if he is falling.

Two Little Pigs

Percy and Porky escaped from their sty
With no one around, they were left high and dry
Into the scrub, they darted with glee
No stopping them now, they want to be free

Into the mud at the side of the dam
Much better here than be bacon or ham
The farmer won't miss them, till coming of night
If he should find them, they'll put up a fight

The gardens the place to head and explore
No good of sending good food to the store
The gate is half open, they're in like a flash
Knocking the gate, it falls with a crash

There's lettuce and cabbage, a beautiful sight
Carrots and parsnips, they're good for a bight
Soon they're so full they lay down to sleep
The farmer comes by then he starts to weep

The sight of the carnage is hard to endure
He turns and heads home, straight for the door
Inside, a shot gun, he loads it in haste
Heads one more for his garden of waste

These two little piggies hurried off home
Each one decides, no more will he roam.
The farmer is off to the market to see
If two little piggies could be used for his tea.

'Ugh' Boots

Ug, as in ugly, ugg boots for free
Who would want them, just wait and see
Worn in the toes, uppers okay
If offered to you, what would you say

Is it the work of a mouse, or is it the toes
Only the owner is the one that knows
She wants to unload, seems that to me
Or a God giving person, she wants to be

The cost of the boots, it's good that it's free
But who could be interested, no, not me
I have a pair exactly the same
Will she swap them for mine, I will if she's game.

Ugly

Ugly, just what does it mean?
Like beauty, it has to be seen.
What is ugly to me, may not be you
But I'm sure it will be, just to a few.

A swamp is a swamp in my list of plans,
Along comes another and calls it wetlands.
The hair on the face, can be black or white
But to me it's just a terrible sight.

A painting, I know, is a beautiful sight,
Graffiti on buildings just doesn't seem right.
Tattoos on the body, I ask this of you
Who wants to see it at age ninety two?

I'm not judge or jury, just stating a fact.
If I were in business I'd probably be sacked.
Be that as it may, we've freedom of speech
I'm not on a box, having to preach.

Uluru

To Uluru, we're heading west
Amid the dust and flies and pests
Alice Springs, they called the place
By Uluru it's been replaced

The lights upon The Rock do play
In reds and browns and even grey
And if you turn your head away
In the distance, more lights at play

Upon The Todd a boat race is run
For guests and locals, lots of fun
But if the rain should fall in town
The runners could surely drown

If in your visit you should see
Gabrielle Wallace wild and free
A talented artist through and through
For Alice Springs is where she grew

Just out of town, Todd homestead lies
A monument to Morse telegraph lines
In eighteen ninety-seven times
World connect to Morse code lines

So, go west, young man, and ladies too
There're stacks of things for you to do
A didgeridoo you could learn to play
Or just freak out. It's all okay.

Up or Down

I wonder where I'm going, is it up, or going down
As I sit and ponder, I always wear a frown
The Good Lord sits there looking well
While the devil smiles in hell

It really is a tug-of-war and the middle one is me
I walk along a tightrope while all I want is flee
Perhaps I should be careful with the company I keep
Instead of following others, like a mob of bleating
    sheep

I'm taking music lessons many times a day
To help me with my sessions, a harp I want to play
Don't want to know of fires, of matches or such
    things
I'll just listen for the calling, when the Master rings

Until the time it happens, it's the waiting game for me
I'll work and toil and wonder, like a working
    bumble bee
And when the word is final, a decision finally made
I know I'll have no option, I hope I make the grade.

Virusitis

We can see now what they do
When they hear of virus flu
Go to their closest store, while there
Leave the racks so clean and bare

Toilet paper, soaps and wipes
Into their trollies, before there's fights
Empties out then back for more
That's the selfish people's law

With the virus, I admit it's bad
But the greedy make me sad
Grabbing all within the stores
Trollies packed out through the doors

More still waiting to go in
Making such a rowdy din
Calls for help from frazzled staff
People pushing, moving fast

When at last the doors are closed
Shelves repacked and specials posed
Tomorrow, be it fine or be it rain
We will do it all again.

Visit Australia

The red back on the toilet seat
You'd think that story can't be beat
But what about the old crocodile
He'd swallow you whole, then he'd smile

Don't get your knickers in a knot
The funnel-web spider, he's got the lot
A bite from him, I will tell
Will send a person straight to hell

If in the water is your thing
Beware the octopus with a ring
He's as deadly with his bite
Against his venom you don't fight

In the grass, he'll wriggle by
But if you should catch his eye
Move on fast, this I beg
Old brown snake might bight your leg

Bees and wasps, as they fly by
May give a sting to unwary eye
But don't forget, as you're having fun
Of the March fly sting in the morning sun.

Australia, with its wildlife things
Lots of love and joy it brings
To those who wants to see our land
And see our creatures, firsthand.

Vote You Must

The vote is on, we've heard the call
It's time to vote, for one and all
There's Labour, in his coat of red
And Liberal blue, the caller said

It matters not if red or blue
This is the thing that you must do
Have your vote and clear the air
For we live in Australia fair

It's half a dozen or six of one
To watch the Polies having fun
Promise the earth but when in power
There's no money left in the tower

But worry not, there's years ahead
When promises can be put to bed
Just put us in, give us a go
Says the wailing cry of old Albo

Then Scomo, with some lessons learned
From him we see the voters turned
His work throughout the covid scare
In hindsight though, his work was fair

The race not run, there's twists and turns
The Independents and Greens will yearn
To put a spoke within the wheels
To put forward their own spiels

But what is new, I hear you ask
The same old things as in the past
The cultured voice of Scomo gone
As Albo's scratchy voice goes on.

Waltzing with Matildas

Waltzing with our football team
Aussies, one and all, it seems
Let the sporting spirits flow
Totally they have the glow

Zero, not the word we know
Into it and let it show
Nothing now to hold us back
Going down the golden track

With our hopes and courage high
It's a case of win or try
Tested are these girls that play
Hope and prayers are what we say

Many times we hold our breaths
At the times that you play best
Till the coming of full time
I'll give you the victory sign

Ladies in the green and gold
Doing things that they are told
As they waltz towards the crowd
Sincerely, girls, you've done us proud.

Weather's Day

The clouds roll in, both black and grey
Thunder roars, as if at play
Sun has gone, he's out of sight
Wind flies in, ready to fight

The once blue sea, now black with rage
Comes once more, as on a stage
Ships at anchor, bob and prance
White capped waves are seen to dance

Our stage is set, the lightning's flash
The cameras roll, we've got a match
Dark clouds cry, the rain drops fall
Sea gulls, high, let out a call

Night rolls in across the land
Is this the way our day was planned
Lightning shows the chaos caused
With wind and storm on collision course.

We Remember

The wars we've had, we remember well
The stories told, we've been to hell
Yet through it all the sun still shines
We remember the better times

Australian men had heard the call
Another country about to fall
Our men in uniform, they go
To fight with friends against the foe

The battles rage, years linger on
Many lives paid and remembered long
The country's proud of efforts made
Memories though, will never fade

As battles rage and heroes are made
Keeping up the Anzac grade
A world at peace we're looking for
A world at war, we want no more.

What is it?

Is it he, she or it? We asked one and other
But I guess though, it really doesn't matter
The attire was odd, to say the least
Might be more at home out at the beach

The shorts, tight fitting, tattered and torn
Not to be considered anything norm
The bra, ill fitting, if that's what it is
A nipple exposed on Bill or is it Liz?

The tummy sticks out, six months at least
Or is it because "it's" just had a feast
A wave or a wink, as it passed me by
Or was "it" just waving away an odd fly

We just looked at each other, mask still in place
Did you see the look on that person's face?
Its mask covered up all but the eyes
We can't make a decision even though we try.

What Pussy Saw

Pussycat, pussycat sleeping so sound
Opened his eyes and look what he found
On his back were nine little chicks
No one else could play such tricks

Looking at them, what can I do?
It's not a meal if I eat one or two
So a mother I'll be to all of the heap
I'm sure they'll follow me just like sheep

It's time for a meal, but what do they eat
Can't see them eating a basin of meat
But just a minute, what is it then?
Along comes mother, a harassed old hen.

What the Lady Saw

We had a lady working, she was working door to
    door
She told us just a little of the strange things that
    she saw
Like the story of the lady who would always live
    alone
The time of the visit, heard a male upon the phone

On another visit, a man came to the door
Said he's the plumber, wore a dressing gown, no
    more
In another unit, there's a party in full swing
No one came to answer, the peeling of the ring

Music was playing as she knocked upon the pane
The weather, bright and sunny, not a sight or rain
Passing down the fence line, heard a closing door
Looking over the fence top, surprised with what
    she saw

A man upon a beach chair, a body in full view
With not a stitch of clothing, what was she to do
Said the sight was sickening, and feeling quite unwell
Came into the office, in sobs she had to tell

The story isn't finished, the hearer quite unfazed
Regarding to your story, the things you have raised
A second call's in order, you could visit there again
The meek and mild young lady held her head in
    shame.

Where am I

I awake from a cold, cold winter's trance
To a warming glow and a quickening glance
A comforting glow, I feel shining on me
Is this the place I wanted to be

I'm welcomed there by friendly folk
But soon I see this is not a joke
The heat's turned on, why won't it stop?
It's got so hot, I'm on the hop

There's friends await, I'm welcome here
Ain't seen them for many a year
A shovel then thrust into my hand
I'm forced to work in the shovel gang

Oh, woe is me, what have I done
I've just met the devil's son
There's rules and rules, you won't believe
From this toil there's no relief

The days go on, night follows too
What is there that I can do
The cast is set, there's no way out
But I have friends galore, about.

Where Did it Go?

Was I going up, or coming down
I not too sure I know
Did I switch it on, or switch it off?
It's really such a blow

It's becoming more the regular
Am I going out, or in?
It doesn't really matter,
But I'm really in a spin

When I'm looking for my glasses
They're up upon my head
And often of a morning
I ask, is this my bed?

I look outside the window
And then behind the door
I seem to look forever
But I'll have to look some more

I don't know what I'm looking for
Or where the hell it is, so
What I want to ask myself
Just, "where did it go?"

Where's My Keeper?

I sit here alone. in my window and weep.
My owner has left me at home in a heap.
She'd boarded me out while she went away.
Left me alone, when I had no say.

She'll be home tonight, I'll give her a fright.
When she comes in, I'll keep well out of sight.
I'll let her think the burglar got me.
She'll have a fit, just wait and see.

I give of my best, when she is at home.
I don't play up or be tempted to roam,
Yet when she goes out, I'm left on the spot,
Weather the weather be cold or be hot.

I'm a one person cat, no interest in males.
I could tell you a lot, but no interest in tales.
I'll sit at the window and watch for my mate
And hope that she hurries, that seems my fate.

Where's Santa?

I hear the children ask " "where's Santa" "?
We have Christmas cake and Fanta,
Lollies, nuts and all things nice
Awaiting now for our Christmas night.

We wait, me and all my relations.
I hope Santa is not in isolation
Will Rudolph and the reindeer team
Be ready for our Christmas dream?

Will he be allowed to cross our border?
Queensland's thoughts should be broader.
Many thoughts have crossed my mind,
But Santa Clause, I want to find.

Does corona affect his reindeer?
This is the problem that I fear.
If they should go into isolation
What will happen within our nation?

Can Santa visit through our chimney?
What's the state of his availability?
Will he drop our presents as he flies by?
If we miss him, many children, I'm sure will cry.

My thoughts for Christmas night is this,
Go to sleep and sleep a night of bliss,
Dream of Santa, corona free
Handing toys to you and me.

Where's the Driver?

On side of a road, I saw such a sight
Mingled, of course, with a touch of fright
A tree growing inside of this car
The car though, won't be going too far

Is there a skeleton, I'd like to know
It's hard to know, for there's nothing on show
Except some gum trees calling it home
I fear the car, no more will it roam

There's trees through the windscreen
More through the roof, from what I've seen
It's life as a car is limited, for sure
Can't even open either side door

The only thing left for this motor car
Having a tree growing, as if in a jar
If you should happen along this way
Stand in the shade and just have a pray.

Whether the Weather

Kissed by the gentle breeze, lay the shining sands
Welcoming the bronzed, sun-tanned body gangs
Soaking up the surf, sea and sun's gentle rays
As they celebrate the long weekend's days

Soon dark clouds appeared on high
Drifting covering clouds over the sky
The surfers then, at a hurried pace
Left for home, as in a race

Thunder roared through the trees
As if chasing after thieves
Lightning flashes to light up the way
To catch the wrongdoers and make them pay

Thunder called yet again, this time in pain
To ask the clouds to bring on the rain
It fell in torrents, soaking the ground
Pools and puddles soon could be found

As thunder growled and lightning flashed
The skies lit up with a mighty crash
A silence then, that all could hear
The heaviest rain throughout the year.

Which Witch

Ding dong, the witch is dead.
She died last night in her witchy bed.
Ran her broom into a tree.
She'd been drinking, but it wasn't tea.

The policeman came upon the scene.
Poor old witch let out a scream.
An ambulance next upon the sight
His crew put up quite a fight.

Off to the hospital she did go
The sight of her was quite a blow.
Arms and legs in splints, for sure
Bandaged head and eyes so sore.

Texted while riding on her broom
Resulted, finally, in her doom.
Riding in our world today,
Eyes on the road or you will pay.

White

White is the snow that gently falls
Covering treetops, roofs, and walls?
White is the snow drop, clean and so fresh
Daintily dancing, in her white, winter dress

White are the clouds, smooth they fly by
Trying to cover a picture blue sky
While down on the ground, the snow lays so deep
And the babes in their cradle, peacefully asleep

Deep in the snow drifts, footprints appear
Showing that the snowman has really been here
Time for the snow plough to clear up the way
So that the children can come out and play

Feathers of snow, still drifting on down
Covering the country and our small English town
Making the countryside ever so white
Peace to the world, for everything's right.

Who is Handicapped?

I watch, in awe, at the Paralympic Games
Then hang my head, to hide my shame
For I've been known to loudly complain
If I get a cramp or my leg's in pain

The athletes here, missing leg or arm
Preform their best without alarm
There're others here, without sight
Into the pool, and how they fight

In wheelchairs, we see the hardy men
Playing football in their den
In basketball they have their pots
Seldom miss with the vital shots

Upon the water, the rowers strain
Forgetting aches and minor pain
Then I watch the swimmers go
No arms, no legs but how they flow

I realize now, that in my life
There's not been the struggle or the strife
Shown by these, "the handicapped one"
It makes me wonder, who has won.

Whoops, Lost Again

Was walking along the beach one day
Had to stop and asked the way
Confused and muddled, I'd become
Wanted to go back home to mum

I took the direction I was shown
Lost my hat, for it was blown
Chased my hat, now which way home
Should have thought to ring my Joan

Called a taxi to take me back
Forgot the address of my flat
To the cop shop, we ended up
They offered tea, I had a cup

Around the town, they drove me
At last a house that I could see
In I went all brash and bold
You're grounded now, I was told.

Who Said That?

Who said that? Who said I'm getting old?
Just because I'm grey and bold
Doesn't mean that I've lost the plot
Up above I've still got the lot

When I walk upon the stairs
I don't take them now in pairs
Just because knees and ankles creak
That does not mean that I am weak

When I go to bed at night
It's just sleep that's in my sight
Though with cramp and pain all night
When I wake, not a pretty sight

My walking now, I take it steady
Does not mean that I'm not ready
I can walk, of this I'm sure
But my feet get quite sore

I don't drop things upon the floor
If I should they're there evermore
My bending now is from the knees
But knees and back quite often freeze

When we were infants way back in time
We had trouble walking but was fine
If I did the same things today
You're getting old, it's what they'd say

If you're the one "who said that"
You're talking through your wide brim hat
Age is just a numbers game
Young or old it's all the same.

Who Stole My Mother?

We arrived by flight from our old home in Greece
Wanted to live in Australia, so free and in peace
The work was hard, and language quite strange
Bought a new home, within our price range

I married, and soon had a home of my own
Talked to my mother each day on the phone
Our family grew up and peace reigned supreme
It worked for us like a slow working dream

The years carried on, mother grew old
Contracted cancer, is what we were told
She has not very long, doctor had said
Only weeks before she was dead

A cremation was held, mourning began
Food was available and use of a band
The family was sad, but life must go on
Her ashes were collected by my darling son

Her ashes were placed 'neath a plant in a pot
Water was sprayed all over the lot
Then placed on the steps at my front door
Thinking it would be there for evermore

Alas, when I awoke and went out the door
My dear mother was with me no more
Some thief in the night, took her away
They'll return her to me, this I do pray.

Who's Zoo?

I went along to the Dubbo Zoo
To spend there just a day or two
Looking at the animals there
Whether they had wool or hair

There were lions and tigers in their cage
The old male lion roared in rage
Cubs and mum took off at speed
Knowing it's time for them to feed

Apes and monkeys were next to view
Resembles someone that I once knew
Mums and babies up in a tree
Gives the impression that they are free

Crocodile out in the muddied pool
He lets you know he's no one's fool
Laying there within the sun
Waiting for his mate and son

Zebra with his coloured coat
Standing near the water's moat
Head up high, he sniffs the air
Then quickly eyes off another pair

Then came upon a grizzly bear
His smell is good but eyesight fair
Looking around for something to eat
As he waddles off on big flat feet

My times nearly over, I've seen some sights
Also saw so many fights
Viewed an elephant, just newly born
But sad to say, not one unicorn.

Will Barrow

Just call me Will, Will Barrow's my name
And a gardener's assistance is my fame
I'm always available, and I'm always on call
Whether it's dust or its rain, I'm having a ball

The sun is my friend, I can work to the end
While others, they go round the bend
If I get heavy, I can do with a push
Or I can be left for a spell near the bush

A hat and the gloves for protection, I must
But use me with care or I'll rust
I'll work day and night, without even a bite
And I don't even put up a fight

At the end of the day, while others pray
I'm put up against a wall, where I stay
And wait for the time I'm wanted again
When I can work all day without gain.

Wind in the Willows

The wind in the willows dance to a tune
Under the light of a silvery moon,
While the waters flow gently over the stones
Emitting sounds like creaks and groans.

The leaves of the willow fall down below
Carried away by the slow moving flow.
Frogs can be heard on the river banks
Croaking away to give of their thanks.

Night birds are calling to distant brood
Eyes alert to the movement of food.
Still is the owl, in the tree top so high
Waiting for insects as they fly on by.

A movement below, the owl's on the flight
He caught movement of a mouse in his sight.
A swoop and the mouse is soon in his beak
The best meal he's had for over a week.

The night is soon over, the moon now at rest.
Things down below, all passed the test.
Morning has broken, the sun shining bright
Most things survived the passing of night.

Witch Night

Last night I went for a ride in the dark
Down the street and twice around the park
Night like pitch, no light was in sight
I ended up with a terrible fright

Ride going freely, a beautiful ride
My little puppy, there by my side
When out of the dark, oh what a sound
I head for the ground, that's where I'm bound

As I hit the ground with no pup in sight
I grab for my broom, I see it's alight
A spark from the engine ignited my broom
What's left now is all doom and gloom.

A long walk home, this I am bound
Of my little puppy, no sight or sound
With broom in hand, a handy tool
I am prepared for any young fool.

Woe is Me

Time on my hands, no thoughts in my head
Been better off, if I had stayed in my bed
But up and about, the sun shining bright
Eggs on toast and the coffee just right

I'm still in lockdown, or that's what they tell
I wander the house, seeing all is well
Then sit in the sun, iPad in hand
Write down a story of just where I stand

Off to the blood place, before I am fed
Not enough iron, the medico said
Now I've a diet of iron stuffed pills
Said that would fix my aches and my ills

Another day passes, I've marked on the wall
The Premier must think I'm having a ball
For the exercise I get, I don't have to pay
From my chair to toilet ten times a day

I'm feeling fine, it's the doctor who knows
What's going on between head and my toes?
It's worrying I know, I go into a rage
When every Doc says "it's only old age".

Wooden Heart

I see upon a battered tree,
Two figures there, for all to see;
He and she, a wooded pair
Enough to make the people stare.

She is naked from the waist,
A shadow there to hide his face.
But as I look through artist eyes
I know a judge would give first prize.

The scene is in the street so wide
She has nothing there to hide.
An African scene, this I know.
She's standing in the morning glow.

Summer heat does not affect.
Winter treats them with respect.
Spring rains to clear the air.
Autumn then to treat them fair.

Words

The English language, our native tongue
In our school it was spelt and sung
As we grew up with our verbs and nouns
Each one with its different sounds

Confusing, I find, for a difficult few
With two, too and the other to, too
Or fore and four, if you want a few more
Then ate and eight, the double of four

Poor old English, or paw and pour
Many a word can make you sore
Or saw your way through a lump of wood
Would make you cry, and so it should

With wind the handle, or wind that blows
It's only the English that really knows
While with the generation of today
It's cool, but is not the cool of yesterday

I shake my head in a confused way
Of the use of English in the present day
The only thing that I'm pleased to say
Most of their talk is by text today.

Working Pet

She sits upon her mobile chair, her doggie by her side
Travelling through the gardens, her dog she shows with pride
Stops to speak with others, of this human race
The dog pulls on the leash, to keep her on the pace

The cheeky little fellow, with love within his eyes
Protects his loving master, at other dogs he flies
But in his tender moments, he watches her with care
And if trouble should attack her, his teeth he will bare

He wags his tail at strangers, sniffs at other pets
If trouble overtakes him, he's off like motor jets
Riding on her mobile she travels far and wide
With her faithful little doggie always by her side.

World Problems

This world of ours cries out in pain
With floods, and fires and drowning rain,
Earthquakes, tsunamis, volcanic ash.
Because of greed and want of cash,

Presidents, Premiers, world leaders all,
Please help out before the fall.
Weathers warming, a heated world.
Grab your flags, let them unfurl.

Take pride with Earth, this land we roam.
Treat this world as you do your home.
Reduce the emissions and carbon gas.
Think of our world, before your cash.

Not contented just to foul up Earth,
Off to Mars for all your worth.
There's many more out there to try
They're just like diamonds in the sky.

For Heaven's sake, and good old Earth,
Get in there and do your worth.
Set this land on a "clean Earth" pace,
Make it fit for our Human Race.

Write On

With the competition on the way
Readers, writers, both will say
It's time to get the writing out
To beat Awesome in this bout

Early works are on the show
Ready now to have a go
Put the pen upon the paper
And come up with a beaut caper

Let the words and para's glow
Settle in and let words flow
Need to keep our record high
Each and every one should try

With our entries light and bright
Chances are we'll win the night
Awesome is the one to beat
So let's turn on Newcastle's heat

Thanks to our intrepid leader
Let her be our checking reader
Earn our club another flyer
Set your goals a little higher.

Writing Verse

When I sit and write in verse
I try to keep it short and terse
Then twist my wrist on my writing hand
Shrug my shoulders that have a tan

Then I stretch my arms and legs
March between set out pegs
Rest my eyes for quite some time
Until I'm feeling right and fine

Another verse then I write
Until my hand is feeling tight
Another stretch and then I say
Dear Lord, help me through the day

It's gonna take me quite a while
Writing in this new found style
Bear with me and you will find
You'll writings nil but back is fine

The lesson with my new found way
If with this you want to stay
Give up writing then, my friend
Back and legs then you can bend.

Yesteryear

I'll tell you a story of long, long ago
When sulkies, horses and drays were the go
Ladies in stays, blouses and skirts
Men in starched collars and pristine white shirts

Horse harnessed and settled into a sulky
Bright clothes and bonnet but nothing too bulky
The man in his britches, braces still showing
Smiles on their faces, their features are glowing

A whinny is heard from the draught horse behind
Awaiting the farmer for his daily grind
The farmer arrives, all battered and worn
Gets on with his work that he started at dawn

The young ones are off, to the glitter of town
To search in the shops for a beautiful gown
An invite was sent, they are expected to be
At the ball, to raise money, for sailors at sea

The farmer, at home, still ploughing the field
Prays for good weather, to increase the yield
Life with its pressures, remain with the old
The young only know, just what they've been told

Life on the land is dicey at best,
To cope with the drought, rabbits and pests
But plod on he must, for life and for health
Perhaps in the end, there may be some wealth.

You Can't Go Back

When I was a lad and in my prime
I was right, the sun would shine
We had fun, just kids in fact
Now I realize, you can't go back

To stay out all night and have a ball
Often happened that I had a fall
Even rode on the local hack
But I know, you can't go back

As a young lad in the local band
Always someone to give a hand
Nothing there for us to lack
But Brother Jack, you can't go back

As a young man, I loved life
Took myself a treasured wife
She passed away, down the track
I'm sorry now, but you can't go back

Friends I've had for many years
They passed on, I've shed some tears
They've left behind a vacant crack
Time has shown you can't go back

Now I'm old and left alone
Seldom a call on the telephone
Legs are tired, skin is slack
Must go forward, you can't go back

When I die and go to where?
I'm sure to find friends waiting there
Whether in white, or dressed in black
There's one thing certain, you can't go back.

You Know

It's strange "you know" what people say,
Whether it be during night or day.
They tell a story, oh so bold
Punctuated with "you know", I'm told.

If, as you say "I know", I ask you this,
With tongue in cheek and full of bliss.
If I know, as you have said
Is there need to go ahead?

You hear it said in all walks of life,
Even from your darling wife.
Just listen to your teachers, bright,
"you know" is taught from toddlers height.

"You know" just makes me really bristle,
Makes me feel like the old scotch thistle.
I wasn't taught to use "you know"
When all is said, I know, you know, I know.

Young Love

Little puppy, small and sweet
Always under mummies feet
Many lessons you must learn
Before a guard dog you must turn

Chase the cat, don't let it in
Keep your eyes on the bikkie tin
Quickly learn the toilet things
Do not bark, when the phone rings

You must learn your masters rules
Do not make any little pools
If you learn these quick and smart
You'll soon win the master's heart

Little puppy, brave and strong
Forget the place you come from
Make this place your very own
Soon you'll win a sheep leg bone.

Zoom

Zoom, is it a plane, a bird or Superman?
No! It's just the new way computer ran
We don't meet people face to face
Things have changed with the human race

We sit at the computer within our home
No need now for us to roam
Our little mouse works over-time
To make sure we all look fine

Log in we must, just to be seen
Upon this great big computer screen
We talk away, when we get the nod
The class is run with an iron rod

Faces we see upon our screen
Background features can be seen
But zoom away while I sit still
Like going backward up a hill

I liked superman and his zoom
Before we have this life of doom
But sit, I must within my house
As quiet as a little church mouse.

www.ingramcontent.com/pod-product-compliance
Lightning Source LLC
Chambersburg PA
CBHW022023290426
44109CB00014B/729